FREEDOM FROM FEAR

HAROLD H. DAWLEY, Jr., Ph.D.

Psychology Service
Veterans Administration Hospital
and
Department of Psychiatry and Neurology
Tulane University School of Medicine
New Orleans, Louisiana

DALE A. GENERAL

Psychology Department
North Texas State University
Denton, Texas
and
Psychology Service
Terrell State Hospital
Terrell, Texas

tempo
books
GROSSET & DUNLAP
A Filmways Company
Publishers • New York

FREEDOM FROM FEAR
Copyright © 1980 by Harold H. Dawley
All Rights Reserved
Interior illustrations by Mike Frazier
ISBN: 0-448-17186-4
A Tempo Books Original
Tempo is registered in the U.S. Patent Office
Published simultaneously in Canada
Printed in the United States of America

PREFACE

Can people be given written material that will help them reduce fear in their lives?

We started looking at this question in 1972, developing a self-directed program for breaking phobic fears. Its initial success formed the basis of the first published report of an effective self-application of systematic desensitization by a hospitalized psychiatric patient.[1] Shortly after, another patient conquered his pervasive fear response using the same material.[2] This case was included in the popular *Relax: How You Can Feel Better, Reduce Stress, & Overcome Tension*[3].

Riding the wave of these initial successes, we wrote the first forerunner of this book, *The Patient's Manual for Systematic Desensitization*,[4] which evolved, as a result of its use with a wide variety of fear problems, into *Self-Directed Systematic Desensitization: A Guide for the Student, Client, and Therapist*,[5] a "do-it-yourself" book for handling common phobias. That year we also came out with a similar self-help guide for conquering social fears, *Achieving Assertive Behavior: A Guide to Assertive Training*.[6]

Over the past few years, these books have been used successfully by a variety of people plagued with the discomfort of unrealistic fears, teaching them new active ways of kicking their fears, cutting down the obstacles and road blocks fear had placed in their way toward becoming the kind of people they wanted to be. They've also been the subject of some very exciting controlled research, with encouraging initial results.[7]

The book you've got in your hand is the culmination of this evolution, the end product of this development toward effective self-directed techniques that you can use to free yourself from social and phobic fears, and the vague general feeling of tension and apprehension so many of us experience in today's world.

Freedom From Fear was written in two sections. The first lays out the *meaning* of fear, what it is, what it does to us, the problems it can create in our minds and bodies and how it comes about in the first place. The second section is dedicated to giving detailed step-by-step instructions you can use to help resist and free yourself from the various kinds of fears that affect us—general anxiety, phobias and social fears—along with a complete set of exercises for achieving deep muscle relaxation. Inventories and progress charts are included at various points as you move through the text, to aid you in identifying problem sources, and in keeping track of your efforts toward breaking your fear responses. Finally, an appendix contains a wide variety of sample hierarchy lists useful in conquering a multitude of different fears.

The techniques presented in the book will help you overcome your fear responses, if you apply them diligently. One thing we've found over the years, is that people who refuse to remain passively in the grips of their fears, who take an active direct role in dealing with their own difficulties, receive an added benefit from applying self-help procedures. They come to believe, more and more strongly in themselves and in their ability to stand up to any problems that may crop up down the road.

We feel that *everybody* has the potential to be this kind of person.

How about *you*?

H.H.D.
D.A.G.

ABOUT THE AUTHORS

Harold H. Dawley, Jr.

Dr. Dawley is a staff psychologist and coordinator of psychological research with the Veterans Administration Hospital in New Orleans, Louisiana, and a clinical assistant professor of psychology in the Department of Psychiatry and Neurology at the Tulane University School of Medicine. His major interest is in the area of behavior therapy with a specific interest in self-help techniques and procedures tobacco smoking and medical psychology. In addition to this book, he has coauthored the *Patient's Manual for Systematic Desensitization: Achieving Assertive Behavior: A Guide to Assertive Training; Self-Directed Systematic Desensitization: A Guide for the Student, Client and Therapist; Achieving Sexual Enhancement; and Friendmanship: How to Make and Keep Friends in An Unfriendly World;* and has published over 30 articles and papers in the area of psychology and behavior therapy. He is a member of the American Psychological Association, Association For Advancement of Behavior Therapy, and is a Clinical Fellow of the Behavior Therapy and Research Society. In 1978 he received the first annual outstanding Psychologist of The Year Award from the Louisiana Psychological Association.

Dale A. General

Dale General received his B. A. degree from Western Michigan University in 1972 and is currently completing a Ph. D. in clinical psychology from North Texas State University. He has served as systems consultant to the Behavior Exchange Clinic, Center for Behavior Studies at North Texas State University and as a writer, editor and production manager for Behaviordelia, Inc. In addition to this book, he has coauthored three other books. *Issues in the Analysis of Behavior; Introduction to the Concepts Of Psychology; and Self-Directed Systematic Desensitization: A Guide for the Student, Client, and Therapist. His current interest are in the area of biofeedback techniques and behavioral medicine.*

ACKNOWLEDGMENTS

Appreciation is expressed to Susan Danahy and Bill Gasparrinni for their thoughtful suggestions for improving this book. Thanks also to Brenda Frost and Kay Rodick for their dedicated typing under unreasonable deadlines. Finally, we must acknowledge our indebtedness to the man whose support and encouragement carried us through our graduate training and subsequent research and professional development, our dear friend, coauthor and fellow colleague, Wes. W. Wenrich, Professor of Psychology at North Texas State University.

**To conquer fear
is the
beginning of wisdom.**

Bertrand Russell

PART ONE

Fear—
What It Is,
How We Learn It,
and What
It Can Do To Us

CHAPTER **ONE**

FEAR
AND
YOU

REALISTIC FEAR

The night was cool but clear, with the stars shining, illuminating the thin wisps of clouds floating gently through the evening sky. Jim Pinkston smiled as he looked at the full moon rising brightly over the dark silhouettes of the downtown skyscraper. He walked toward the small corner grocery for a pack of gum, as he'd done often before on pleasant evenings.

They can say anything they want about it, he thought. Crime, poverty. . .I still like the city. Guess I always will.

As he approached the store, he could hear the faint ringing of the cash register within, keys moving under the withered hands of the old man who ran the place. But entering the door, Jim sensed a disturbing change, a stillness, a foreboding silence. Puzzled, he turned toward the check-out counter, and froze in this tracks when he saw a large man shakily holding a gun in the owner's pale, frightened face.

"Empty that till into the sack, old man, 'fore I blow you apart!"

5

As the owner began filling the sack with money, Jim moved silently up behind the thief grabbing a large can from a shelf. He swung the can against the man's head with all the strength he could muster, knocking the thief to the floor, unconscious. Jim quickly grabbed the gun and, holding it to the man's neck, yelled for the owner to call the police. Only then did he notice the blood pumping in his ears, his heart racing, and his breath coming in quick gasps. It was as if he could feel every nerve in his body standing on edge. Whew! he thought: I haven't felt like this since the army. . .

FEAR: icy, tingling, paralyzing, terrifying. We've all felt its cool fingers grab us from time to time during our lives. Brushes with death or injury, the horrors of war, diseases and painful experiences, all cause fear to varying degrees. We all know what it feels like, but what actually is fear, and why does it exist?

Fear is a very old, very basic pattern of human response you might call a "defense-alarm" system, passed down from our ancestors over eons of biological evolution. And it serves a very basic function for us: Fear prepares us for emergencies, *allowing us to fight or run at maximum power*.

Briefly and simply, here's how it works. When we perceive a threat to ourselves, our brain sends a signal through the nervous system to our adrenal glands. These glands react, releasing a variety of chemicals into our blood, causing a rapid and dramatic change— our body gets ready to *fight* or *run*. Our rate of breathing goes up, along with our heartbeat and blood pressure. There's also a slowing down of the digestive process, a shifting away of blood from the stomach and intestines to the heart and muscles, along with an elevation of blood sugar levels and an increase in the number of red corpuscles, allowing the blood to carry more oxygen. Other chemical changes begin, making the blood clot more easily. Passages to the lungs open wider permitting greater amounts of air to be inhaled, and changes may occur in the pupils of the eyes, allowing more light to enter. The collective purpose of all these changes is simply this: to make us ready to function at *maximum power*. In short, fear "fine-tunes" the body for peak operation, automatically and efficiently, all in a matter of seconds.

We all experience these changes in pretty much the same way: Heart thumping, sweating, faster breathing—maybe even a gasping for air—loss of appetite, nausea, muscle twitches. These feelings can range from an uneasy dread to a full-blown, paralyzing panic, depending on the person and situation.

This defense-alarm system serves a critical role in our survival as individuals and as a species. As we saw in the example of Jim Pinkston at the start of this chapter, the fear response helps us get through emergency situations, fleeing, or struggling and fighting with a strength and power that wouldn't be possible otherwise. These changes are, in a very real sense, lifesaving at times. Stories abound of people just like you and me running amazing distances at unbelievable speeds, lifting incredible weights, literally moving mountains to save themselves or loved ones. And it takes only a minute's thought to see how these massive bursts of strength must have helped our ancient ancestors survive in a time when extreme danger from deadly animals and the ravagings of unmerciful elements were everyday events.

Yes, fear in the face of *real danger* can be critical for us humans. But let's turn our attention to a few other types of situations where the fear response may be more an enemy than a friend.

UNREALISTIC FEARS

"I know its silly, Roger, but I can't get into that thing... you know that. Why do you keep insisting?"

"Margie, the lawyer's office is on the twenty-second

floor! Please. Just try it. I'll be with you. . .really, there's nothing to be scared of."

"Okay. . .I'll try. Oh, Roger, I can't do it. . .I can't!"

"Sure you can, honey. This is the safest elevator in the city. Let's just step right in here. . "

"Let me out, please! Roger, I'm getting sick! I can't do it! Please. . .I can't breath!"

"Okay, okay! Margie, I'm trying to be patient, but we've got to do something. You can't go on like this. You can't avoid elevators for the rest of your life."

"I know. I'm sorry, Rog, I really am. But I can't help it. You don't know what it's like. . .I can't help it. . ."

Margie and Roger Appleton. A couple with very few problems in their lives, except this one: Margie can't bring herself to get into an elevator. This didn't matter where they used to live. But it sometimes creates problems since they've arrived in New York City. When faced with an elevator, Margie breaks out in a sweat, begins to tremble, and feels faint and nauseous. And, she can't help herself, in spite of all the trouble this causes them. Margie Appleton has an elevator phobia.

* * *

John Klien shook his head sadly as he looked at his new television. This is really absurd. . .I can't go through my whole life this way. Why can't I do it?

He looked at the electric cord, moving his eyes slowly from the set, down the length of the cord to the large black plug on the end. The empty electrical outlet waited—silent, mocking.

John's eyes darted around the small room—looking for something to give him the strength he needed to carry out the seemingly simple task at hand. He found nothing.

"Hell with it," he said "I'm gonna do it."

His hand shook as he moved to pick up the snakelike TV cord. He pulled it slowly toward the outlet, closer and closer. . .then he dropped the cord from his hand suddenly, as if it had burned him. He ran into the kitchen and leaned against the counter, straining to calm the fear welling up inside. The outlet remained empty. John had failed again.

Like Margie with elevators, John has a "phobia" about electricity, a phobia that has grown to include electric devices of all sorts. They make him feel anxious and tense, even though he knows they can't really hurt him. He just can't bring himself to do much of anything that involves electric current. It causes him many problems, and he can't help it. John has an electricity phobia.[1]

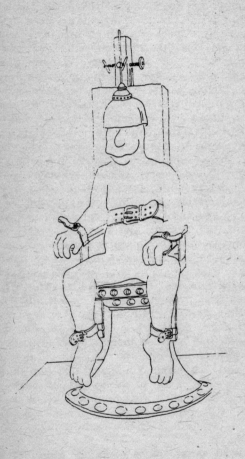

And to think... I used to be afraid of electrical appliances!

PHOBIAS

There's an important difference between the fear we saw in the Jim Pinkston example and these situations. In Jim's case, his arousal helped him deal with the thug trying to rob the store. Without it, Jim may not have been able to knock him out cold with just one blow. His fear provided the extra emergency power he needed *right then*, quite possibly saving Jim's life, not to mention the shop owner's. But in the elevator and TV set examples, you see how our arousal system can get in the way, as like when we're tuned for "fight or flight" and there's no threat, no real danger. Sad but true, many folks walk around fully mobilized and tense most of the time. All of the crises powers are exploding inside us, there's nothing to fight and nowhere to run. Uptight, wired, nervous, tense—whatever you want to call it, it boils down to the same thing: an uncomfortable, disrupting sort of arousal.

Being afraid of any angry doberman lunging at your throat is one thing. But what about a fear of being alone? Of heights or harmless snakes? Fear in the first case is realistic and useful. In the others, however, it's unrealistic, serving only to block out goals, and limit our horizons. We often label the fear we feel in harmless situations "irrational," or maybe even "silly." After all, nothing here can really hurt us. When such persistent, unrealistic fears are caused by *specific* things or events, they're called *phobias*. Phobias aren't any less disturbing just because there aren't any "logical" reasons to be afraid. For Margie Appleton, the prospect of an elevator ride is about as appealing as the cold barrel of a pistol pressed against her neck. And for John Klien, the thought of even a mild electric shock packs nearly as much fear as the thought of a head-on collision.

Phobias are quite common. Many of us have unrealistic fears of one kind or another; they come in all shapes and sizes. If you can name it, chances are pretty

Honestly Harold, I don't know why you're getting so upset about a silly little spider!

good there's someone who fears it. Here's a list of common phobias:

Fear of being alone
Fear of darkness
Fear of hospitals
Fear of injections
Fear of crossing streets
Fear of sexual intercourse
Fear of thunder
Fear of crossing bridges
Fear of riding in cars, buses or subways
Fear of bugs and insects
Fear of birds
Fear of dirt
Fear of sick people
Fear of dead people
Fear of dead animals
Fear of rodents
Fear of cemeteries
Fear of lightning
Fear of flying
Fear of open spaces
Fear of riding in elevators
Fear of being watched
Fear of cats
Fear of spiders
Fear of crowds
Fear of water
Fear of taking tests
Fear of eating in crowded restaurants
Fear of visiting doctor or dentist

Fortunately, some very effective ways of breaking loose from phobic fear have been developed, and we'll discuss them in detail a little later. But now, let's turn our attention to another kind of unrealistic but common form of fear.

SOCIAL ANXIETY
The air was alive with the sounds of ice clinking in glasses, lively music, laughter and conversation. The office party was well under way, being for many a

welcomed chance to break loose from the ol' routine and have a little fun.

But not so for David Smith. No, for David it was torturous, fear-producing and yet another chance to fail socially. He sat alone on the couch, away from the crowd, staring into the pitiful remains of a Scotch and water (his fourth), silently wishing he hadn't come.

Why can't I be like them? Just for once, to talk, laugh, just to be normal...awww, it's no use. I wouldn't be able to think of anything to say...just make a fool of myself, as usual...

Just the thought of getting up and talking to someone made David tense up. His palms began to sweat; his mouth became dry as a bone. He tilted the glass to his lips, downing the rest of his drink, the cool liquid soothing his parched throat. Just then, a soft voice jolted him from his thoughts, pulling him back to the party.

"Hi. I'm Julie, Who're you?"

"Uh, David S-Smith."

"Well, hello David Smith," the young lady said, a coy smile dancing on her lips. "I've seen you around the office, but you always look so busy...never thought I'd get the chance to talk to you. Some party, eh?" She tried to look David in the eye, but he continued to stare at his empty glass.

David felt a trickle of sweat roll down his back, felt his face begin to redden, and noticed his hands were starting to tremble as he tried desperately to think of something, anything, to say. Something clever, witty, charming, intelligent. But he couldn't. He just sat there, in a slowly growing panic, wishing he could get up and run. He became so aware of his own fear that he lost track of what Julie was saying.

"...but who knows...maybe it won't be as hot this summer as it was last year."

"Wha.. uh.. .yea, who knows," he mumbled nervously, thinking to himself, Boy, was that ever an

intelligent remark!

Julie now looked around the room, having failed to even catch David's eye. *"Yes, well. . .oh, there's Mary. Excuse me, David, I need to talk to her. It was. . .uh. . . nice talking to you. See ya."*

"Yea, see ya."

David clumsily made his way over to the bar, feeling flustered and embarrassed wishing he were invisible. *Well, nice going, social butterfly. Now there's one more person out there who sees the real you. A zero. Zip. A nobody. Won't I ever change?*

David Smith. A good-looking guy in his mid-twenties, intelligent, well-read, earning good money. But in social gatherings, David falls apart, mumbling when spoken to, answering questions in monosyllables, slinking off into a corner to absorb himself in some magazine or painting on the wall. David was well on his way toward becoming a social recluse, a modern-day troll, living out his life under the bridge of his own fear. Luckily, he sought out help.

It was obvious, almost from the start of my work with David that his social fears centered around his absolute dread of saying or doing something "wrong," or "stupid." So we concentrate on two things: having David realize that it's not the end of the world if he says or does something dumb from time to time and developing his social skills, with an emphasis on teaching him how to start a conversation, keep it going and stop it, with *confidence*.

David's far from alone under his "bridge." Many of us are victims of our social fears. We're afraid of offending someone, afraid people won't like us once we've opened our mouths and shown them what "fools" we "really" are, afraid to express our feelings and opinions, afraid to open ourselves to an honest interaction with someone else. Usually, a bunch of social fears operate together to sabotage our exchanges with others. These may include, for example:

A fear of initiating a conversation
A fear of maintaining control of a conversation
A fear of speaking loud enough
A fear of extemporaneous talking
A fear of emotional honesty and "feeling" talk
A fear of saying "I like you"
A fear of saying "I'm sorry"
A fear of admitting a mistake
A fear of talking about oneself
A fear of using the personal pronoun "I"
A fear of agreeing with compliments
A fear of giving compliments
A fear of disagreeing
A fear of asking "Why?"
A fear of making requests
A fear of saying "No"
A fear of ending a conversation
A fear of leaving a group
A fear of taking a stand
A fear of admitting weakness or fear
A fear of being criticized
A fear of applying for a job
A fear of asking for a deserved advancement
A fear of asking for a date
A fear of physical closeness
A fear of maintaining eye contact
A fear of showing facial expression

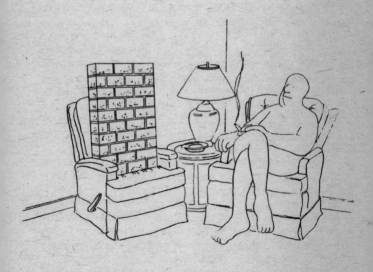

Frankly, Mildred, you're not the easiest person in the world to talk to!

A common denominator among all these fears is, of course, a fear of rejection. So it was with David. And, like David, socially fearful people tend to inhibit their normal desires. For the most part, they're quiet individuals, passive rather than active, followers rather than leaders. And, because of their fear of speaking out, they let themselves be taken advantage of, allowing others to "work them over" time and time again, at the cost of their self-esteem.

The degree of social fear and anxiety naturally varies from one individual to the next. Most of us encounter some types of situations where we feel unusually tense. What teenager, for instance, doesn't get "butterflies" at the prospect of the first date? And who among us hasn't felt stagefright before giving a talk—even in front of a small friendly group?

What about you? While waiting in line, have you ever had anyone cut ahead of you, resented it, yet been to timid to speak out? Do you feel intimidated by snooty waiters in fancy restaurants who give you indifferent service? And are you then afraid they'll think you're a cheap slob is you leave less than a "good" tip? Do people make ridiculous demands on you that you're unable to refuse even though you want to? Do you feel awkward in situations that require you to talk to strangers? Are you bad at small talk? If so, you're not alone. Far from it.

If it's just snooty waiters or pushy line-crashers that make you uncomfortable, then at least your life isn't limited to any major degree. But if you're like David, a person who experiences an intense dread that clouds most of your social contacts and so restricts your life, then almost any gathering of people can trigger your fear. Phobic people can usually manage to avoid their phobic objects, and thus, their anxiety. But not the socially anxious. They're nearly always in a state of arousal. People and social exchanges are everywhere, constant, unavoidable. And the truly unfortunate thing about social anxiety is that it's so handicapping in today's world. It blocks many of our goals, cutting to the core of our self-worth, seriously affecting how we see ourselves relative to others, causing potentially successful people to meet failure again and again, ultimately leading to self-doubt, isolation, loneliness, and despair.

A grim picture? Not if you want to change. Because like phobic fear, social anxiety can be beaten. And later, we'll see how.

FREE-FLOATING FEAR

Gerald didn't have the slightest idea why he felt like he did. A sinking feeling in the pit of his stomach, cool and sweaty palms, a nearly constant sensation of overwhelming dread, Gerald was uptight nearly all the time. And he didn't know why. After all, he sure wasn't what anybody would call a failure. At thirty-five, he was happily married with two healthy sons, successful in his job as an accountant, had no money problems and others seemed to like him. He wasn't an aggressive, obnoxious type of guy, going through life walking all over other people's toes. Quite the opposite, in fact. A quiet, inoffensive, slightly withdrawn person, Gerald often went out of his way to keep from saying or doing something that might bother someone else.

But for years, a multitude of vague fears plagued him, like intangible ghosts he couldn't quite put his finger on, filling him with arousal and keeping him from fully enjoying the life he'd built for himself. Why, he asked himself constantly, searching in vain for a way to solve the misery that so dominated his life. But he found no answers, no solutions, no explanations, continuing helplessly to live in fear, a victim to his own dread.

Arousal or tension that seems to go on and on, day in, day out, regardless of what's happening around you is called *free-floating fear*. It's different from the kinds of fears we've already talked about, because it's not "tied" to anything in particular. Realistic fears are set off by threats to our safety. Phobias by some thing or event, and social fears by people and people-type situations. But free-floating fear just keeps on coming, no matter what's going on, making us feel uncomfortable and tense most of the time, eating away bit by bit from our full enjoyment of life. But this kind of fear can be broken also if you have the will to change it.

So, we see there're basically four types of fear. One realistic, three unrealistic. One helpful to our lives, three that block our goals, hurdles in the way of our becoming the kinds of folks we'd like to be. Phobias, social fears and free-floating arousal plague many of us, affecting our lives for so long that we may even start to take them for granted, looking at them as "just one of those things," accepting their bothersome effects as an unavoidable byproduct of modern life. But this kind of thinking is the *first* thing you've got to get rid of if you're ever going to break the fear habit. Unrealistic fears are *not* something you just have to live with. They're *not* unavoidable or unsolvable byproducts of life in the twentieth century. They *are* beatable, *if* you have the drive, desire, willingness and perseverance to apply the things we're going to lay out for you in this book. No longer will you have to say "I know it's silly, but I'm still afraid." You *can* break the fear habit!

WHAT ARE YOUR FEARS?

Below, we've included a form that will help you identify the kinds of fears that may be bothering you, blocking your way to happiness. To the right of each item, you'll find a series of numbers, from 1 through 5. Circle the number that comes closest to matching the amount of anxiety you feel associated with the items. The number 1 refers to no anxiety; 5 to extreme anxiety; with 2 through 4 representing small to fairly great amounts.

Only circle *one* anxiety number for each item.

FEAR LEVEL

1 NONE	2 A LITTLE	3 A FAIR AMOUNT	4 A LARGE AMOUNT	5 EXTREME EXTREME

TYPE	ITEM	FEAR LEVEL
S/P	1. Making a public speech* ✓	1 2 3 4 5
P	2. Flying*	1 2 3 4 5
P	3. Elevators*	1 2 3 4 5
S/P	4. Applying for a Job* ✓	1 2 3 4 5
S/P	5. Walking into a crowded room*	1 2 3 4 5
P	6. Crossing streets*	1 2 3 4 5
S/P	7. Riding in a crowded subway* ✓	1 2 3 4 5
P	8. Crossing bridges*	1 2 3 4 5
S	9. Lull in conversation*	1 2 3 4 5
S	10. Being watched by others* ✓	1 2 3 4 5
P	11. Riding in a car*	1 2 3 4 5
P	12. Visiting the dentist*	1 22 3 4 55
S/P	13. Being alone*	1 2 3 4 5
P	14. Open spaces*	1 2 3 4 5
S/P	15. Strangers*	1 2 3 4 5
P	16. Riding in a train* ✓	1 2 3 4 5
P	17. Visiting the physician*	1 2 3 4 5
P	18. Harmless insects (spiders, cockroaches, etc.)*	1 2 3 4 5
P	19. Riding in a bus*	1 2 3 4 5
P	20. Water (swimming)*	1 2 3 4 5
S	21. Expressing anger	1 2 3 4 5
S/P	22. Crowds* ✓	1 2 3 4 5
P	23. Harmless snakes and reptiles*	1 2 3 4 5

FEAR LEVEL

1 NONE	2 A LITTLE	3 A FAIR AMOUNT	4 A LARGE AMOUNT	5 EXTREME EXTREME

TYPE	ITEM	FEAR LEVEL
S	24. Authority figures (Supervisor, Boss, etc.)	1 2 3 4 5
S/P	25. Losing control ✓	1 2 3 4 5
S	26. Looking foolish	1 2 3 4 5
P	27. Storms* ✓	1 2 3 4 5
P	28. Darkness*	1 2 3 4 5
P	29. Cemeteries*	1 2 3 4 5
P	30. Small enclosed rooms*	1 2 3 4 5
S	31. Making requests	1 2 3 4 5
P	32. Cats*	1 2 3 4 5
S	33. Looking other people in the eye	1 2 3 4 5
P	34. Knives, or other sharp objects	1 2 3 4 5
P	35. Birds	1 22 3 4 5
P	36. Dogs*	1 2 3 4 5
S/P	37. Taking a test or examination*	1 2 3 4 5
P	38. Guns ✓	1 2 3 4 5
S	39. Being rejected	1 2 3 4 5
S	40. Expressing affection	1 2 3 4 5
S	41. Greeting others	1 2 3 4 5
P	42. Receiving an injection*	1 2 3 4 5
S	43. Asking for a date ✓	1 2 3 4 5
S	44. Saying "No" to a request ✓	1 2 3 4 5
P	45. Fire ✓	1 2 3 4 5
P	46. Looking down from high places* ✓	1 2 3 4 5

*See Appendix I for sample anxiety-stimulus hierarchies (pp. 185) for these fears.

FEAR LEVEL

1 NONE	2 A LITTLE	3 A FAIR AMOUNT	4 A LARGE AMOUNT	5 EXTREME EXTREME

TYPE	ITEM	FEAR LEVEL
S	47. Disagreeing with others	1 2 3 4 5
S/P	48. Sexual intercourse	1 2 3 4 5
S	49. Making small talk	1 2 3 4 5
P	50. Electrical appliances	1 2 3 4 5
S	51. Asking "Why?"	1 2 3 4 5
P	52. People with physical deformities	1 2 3 4 5
S	53. Being interrupted	1 2 3 4 5
P	54. Sick people	1 2 3 4 5
S/P	55. Eating in crowded restaurants*	1 2 3 4 5
S	56. Starting conversations	1 2 3 4 5
S/P	57. Becoming nauseous	1 2 3 4 5
S	58. Expressing your emotions ✓	1 2 3 4 5
P	59. People who seem "insane" ✓	1 2 3 4 5
S	60. Agreeing with compliments	1 2 3 4 5
P	61. Seeing others receive an injection	1 2 3 4 5
P	62. Dead animals	1 2 3 4 5
S	63. Talking about yourself	1 2 3 4 5
S	64. Being physically touched by others	1 2 3 4 5
S/P	65. Nude men	1 2 3 4 5
S/P	66. Nude women	1 2 3 4 5
P	67. Blood	1 2 3 4 5
S	68. Ending conversations	1 2 3 4 5
S	69. Smiling, or other facial expressions of emotions	1 2 3 4 5

FEAR LEVEL

1 NONE	2 A LITTLE	3 A FAIR AMOUNT	4 A LARGE AMOUNT	5 EXTREME EXTREME

TYPE	ITEM	FEAR LEVEL
P	70. Dirt	1 2 3 4 5
S/P	71. Being in charge of others	1 2 3 4 5
S	72. Failure	1 2 3 4 5
S	73. Being ignored	1 2 3 4 5
S	74. Paying compliments to others	1 2 3 4 5
S	75. Feeling disapproved of	1 2 3 4 5
P	76. Prospect of a minor operation ✓	1 2 3 4 5
S	77. Making mistakes	1 2 3 4 5
P	78. Being in a boat	1 2 3 4 5
S	79. Being teased	1 2 3 4 5
S	80. Expressing love	1 2 3 4 5

Other Fears (Write in any additional fears)

1 2 3 4 5

1 2 3 4 5

1 2 3 4 5

1 2 3 4 5

1 2 3 4 5

1 2 3 4 5

1 2 3 4 5

*See Appendix I for sample anxiety-stimulus hierarchies (pg. 185) for these fears.

After rating each fear item, take note of all those you rated above *3*—the ones that cause you to feel a large amount or extreme amount of fear. These are the fears you'll probably want to concentrate on breaking, at least as a start.

The "type" column to the left of each item tells you the general category each fear falls into: *S* refers to social fears; *P* to phobic; and S/P to fears that involve a blending of social and phobic elements. This "coding" tells you which chapter or chapters you'll need to concentrate particularly hard on in conquering your specific fears. But keep in mind that the categories of fears *blend into* each other. The distinction is often a fairly hazy one, a soft, muted grey rather then black and white. So you may want to draw from the whole range of techniques we talked about in *Part Two: Breaking Loose From Unrealistic Fear,* rather than limiting yourself to just one chapter.

But before getting into the ways of reducing fear, let's learn a little more about its effects on us, how we cope with it, and how we learn to fear in the first place.

CHAPTER TWO

FEAR,
HEALTH
AND
COPING

In the last chapter, we looked at the different faces of fear, the help it can provide, and the hinderances it can put into our lives. We saw the obstacles unrealistic fear places in our path toward becoming the kinds of people we wish to be, the limitations it can set on our happiness. Now, let's take a look at what long-term bouts with unrealistic fear can do to our health.

CHRONIC FEAR AND YOUR HEALTH
Simply, arousal kept up over a long period of time has harmful effects on our bodies. When fear and stress are maintained over time, we call it *chronic* arousal. Doctors estimate that about half of the people coming in to see them have health problems caused at least partly by chronic and intense emotional arousal—*one person out of two.* A disturbingly high percentage, really. The fact of the matter is, chronic stress can and does kill people.

In today's jet-paced world, more people than ever before find themselves falling victims to chronic stress, running helter-skelter from meeting to meeting, place to place, task to task, without stopping to catch their breath. And the ultimate reward for their efforts? The Golden Carrot dangling in front of their noses, the treasure they've been chasing all these hard and hurried years? Well many folks get it, all right. But they often find that the pot of gold at the end of the rainbow is somehow less enjoyable now that they're nursing ulcers or heart problems picked up along the way. Life in the fast lane takes its toll on our bodies, and may finally put us in the junkyard, burned-out heaps, rusted through by the effects of chronic stress.

FEAR AND YOUR HEART
Probably the strongest, most solid and steadfast piece of equipment we have is our heart. This little ticker has a massive job to do, pumping life-giving blood through the miles of vessels inside us from our start as a person

till our death, not daring to take a minute's rest. Like an inner mailman, the heart must carry on, through thick and thin, because if it stops, it's curtains for us. Today, heart problems are on the increase, probably because of our fast, reckless life-styles. One of the factors most closely related to coronary disease is the chronic arousal of the *fear response*. When coupled with the high-fat, junk-food diets many of us are on and a lack of consistent exercise, chronic fear and stress take on even more important roles in making our hearts fall down on the job.

Fear, as we saw in the first chapter, revs up to fight or run. But when we do neither, walking around with our motors running at full speed but our transmission in neutral, the changes produced in our inner working can do real damage. For instance, fear causes our blood viscosity to increase. This simply means our blood will clot quicker than normal. Nice thing to have if you're bleeding from wounds. But if you aren't, it means your blood's going to have a harder time flowing through narrowed coronary or cerebral arteries, making you heart work all the more, maybe even causing damage to several other parts of your body, the parts not getting the blood they need to stay healthy.

Your heart is just like any other organ, muscle, or machine for that matter. It has a finite number of beats in it. So, in general, the harder it has to work, or the longer it's strained with unusually heavy loads, the sooner it'll wear out.

We'll show you what we mean. In a group of 100 heart patients considered in a study, 91% (that's nine out of ten) were suffering from chronic stress. Further, 70% smoked 30 or more cigarettes a day and 53% were on high-fat diets. Comparing these figures with those of a group of folks having healthy hearts, the researchers found that only 20% of the healthy group were under chronic stress, 35% smoked and 20% were on high fat diets.[2]

The numbers speak for themselves. What they're saying is that chronic fear is bad for your heart. And what's bad for your heart is bad for you.

FEAR AND YOUR BREATHING

Carl squinted at the bright sun through the face guard of his football helmet and felt the breeze blowing gently across the field, cooling the sweat on his face. When he'd gotten up that morning and saw what a nice day it was going to be for the big game, he was almost sorry.

Now I'll have no excuse if I screw up, he thought.

Looking up now at the smiling faces of his parents in the stands, he remembered his father's words the night before. "Now tomorrow's the big day, Carl. I don't have to tell you how much the team's depending on you to get them through. And you know how proud your Mother and I are of you out there. So get in there and win!"

The score was thirteen to seventeen, the opposition having the lead. Carl's team had the ball on the fifteen yard line, fourth down, twenty seconds left in the game. It was a touchdown now, or lose. Carl was to run a pattern into the end zone, shaking the defense to clear a path for the TD pass.

Digging in, Carl heard the call, felt the snap and dashed out his pattern. It worked, leaving him alone in the end zone. The pass from the quarterback came hard and fast, hitting him perfectly, right on the numbers. Carl wrapped himself around the ball as he had done so many times before, but this time, it slid from his fingers! He dove, frantically, desperately, stretching to get the slippery pigskin before it hit the ground. It didn't work.

Pass incomplete.

Over the cheers for the opposing team's victory, Carl's teammates tried to console him. But Carl couldn't hear them. He lay on the turf, gasping for breath, a vise tightening around his chest, lungs filled with cotton, constricted into a ball that refused to allow air to enter. It was the worst asthma attack he'd ever had.

Carl was a client referred to me because of chronic anxiety, a variety of muscle tics and spasms, and asthma. He was twelve at the time, and a bright, friendly youngster successful in both school and sports. But inside Carl was forever aroused, trying desperately to live up to the often unrealistic expectations of his folks, fighting a war he'd never win. His mother and father were caring and loving parents, but they put strong demands on Carl to succeed in everything he did. When Carl's doctor couldn't find any medical cause for his problems and recommended therapy, they were amazed, seeing no connection between what they were doing and Carl's distress. But, through therapy, we reduced many of Carl's fears, his parents became aware of their role in his problem and his physical symptoms gradually went away.

Besides asthma, several other respiratory problems are related to fear arousal. Emphysema and hay fever symptoms, for instance, become worse when fear is present, and diminish when we're relaxed. So like the heart, our breathing can suffer due to chronic stress or fear.

FEAR AND YOUR SKIN

Getting "goose pimples," turning "cold with fear:" We've all heard those expressions used by people to describe the fear response. The fact is, fear can have a mild to serious effect on the skin. When a sample of active members of the American Dermatological Association were asked whether they thought excessive fear or emotional reactions are important in the development of skin problems, nearly all of them answered *yes*.[3]

Fear causes a variety of skin disorders, like rashes, hives, dermatitis and itching. Acne, the heartbreaking plight of many youngsters, is also intimately related to chronic fear and stress. Aging, as shown by changes in the face and graying of the hair, can happen early as a result of prolonged stress. Everyone has seen this effect, watching someone grow old "before their time." If you look at photos of our presidents before and after their terms in office, you'll see dramatic evidence of the relationship between stress and aging.

FEAR AND YOUR GASTROINTESTINAL SYSTEM

"It scared the crap out of me." An earthy but accurate way of describing how fear affects your gastrointestinal system. "Butterflies" in your stomach, nausea, cramps and diarrhea, all commonly result from intense or longlasting fear. We seem to handle fear like we handle poison, strange as it sounds. With both, there's a decrease in the stomach's putting out of acid and an increase in mucus secretion. Similar changes happen in the digestive tract. The result? Vomiting, stomach aches and diarrhea.

Chronic stress may also cause more serious problems in our gastrointestinal tract, as we see in the case of John Evans.

John Evans was a man with a mission. His wife had been in the hospital for the last year and a half fighting against death, and here he was fighting against life. Mary's illness was an expensive one, and no matter how hard he tried, he couldn't convince his five kids that they really didn't have to eat to stay alive.

So John Evans had to hustle. And hustle.

During the day he taught high school drafting. At night he was a guard for the Acme Warehouse. It was notoriously underguarded, but the pay was good.

It was great for the first month. Well, not exactly great, but things were quiet and John had a fair amount of time during his watch when he could grade his students' drawings. He was doing fine, except for rarely seeing the kids.

And then the break-ins started.

"There were three of 'em," he remembered telling the guard who found him knocked unconscious. "They snuck up on me, I guess. I just saw them for a second before I got hit. . .I don't remember much after that." John was lying. The thieves had taken him by surprise while he was dozing. He never knew what hit him. They had gotten away with about five thousand dollars worth of equipment.

Things got worse for John. His performance at school was on the decline, papers were backed up, he had little time to sleep and those short breaks of slumber he did get were racked with nightmares. The kids needed new clothes and he didn't have the money to buy them, but the warehouse was the worse part. There had been seven break-ins in as many months and the guards were getting edgy. John didn't sleep on the job anymore. Quite the contrary. He could feel his stomach begin to churn as soon as he drove up to the place. Sometimes it hit as soon as he got in the car to leave. He started to notice a change in the way he felt, especially during the day. He was weak, lightheaded and his stomach burned with a unique kind of fire. Even though John didn't eat much, he was never hungry, and he began to drop weight like a fat man in a steam bath.

Then it happened. While at school, the hospital had called saying that Mary had taken a turn for the worse. A student found John lying on the floor by his desk, his face a singular shade of white.

At the hospital, the doctors discovered that John had developed severe ulcers in his stomach and had been bleeding internally for some time. These little holes were the result of the chronic stress in his life, a stress that nearly killed him.

Luckily, with some medical help and a little counseling, John was able to change his life-style, slowing down, relaxing, putting things in their proper perspective and still make the kind of living he needed. His ulcers improved, as did the condition of his wife. But had he continued his old life-style, running wildly through the days and months, he may never have lasted to enjoy Mary's new health.

FEAR AND OTHER PROBLEMS

Chronic fear and stress may cause other physical problems in addition to the ones we've discussed here. Migraine headaches, muscle cramps and tremors, lower back pain, insomnia, heightened reactions to allergies, hypertension (high blood pressure), constipation, colitis, sexual problems like impotency and frigidity—all can be produced or intensified by unchecked, chronic arousal. We don't mean to say these are *always* produced by fear, but we do want to point out that fear can and does have effects on your body that may have damaging results in the long run, increasing your doctor bill, maybe even decreasing your life-span. And let's face it. . .who needs that?

COPING WITH FEAR: DRUGS, ALCOHOL, AND AVOIDANCE

The thin, drawn figure crept slowly along the dark tenement stairway, looking back over his shoulder every few seconds as if watching for someone. At the top of the stairs, he entered a dark room, barren except for a mattress in one corner, pillows strewn about the floor, a sink, a small refrigerator and an ancient hot plate. A single light bulb hanging from the ceiling lit the pale, sunken face of the man, illuminating with harsh clarity the worn lines in his forehead, the dark bags under his darting, feverish eyes.

From his shabby overcoat, he produced a small bag of white powder. Turning on the hot plate, he placed a burnt spoon on one of the burners and pulled an eyedropper and hypodermic syringe from his pocket. After holding the needle over a burning match, the man placed a few drops of water into the hot spoon, along with an amount of the white powder. Once mixed, the solution was drawn into the syringe. Hands shaking, he drew his thin belt around his arm, just above the elbow, pulling it tightly until the veins in his inner forearm stood out, anticipating what was to come. The needle pierced the swollen vein with practiced precision, and once the belt was released, the solution mixed with the blood flowing within, joining in its journey through the body, finally hitting the brain.

With a sigh, the man fell back slowly onto a pillow, fingers relaxing their grip on the needle, his sunken eyes narrowing into slits, seeing nothing, his ears oblivious to the sounds of the street below. . .

* * *

Harry Jackson watched television in his darkened den, enjoying the numbing feeling he was beginning to get as he nursed his sixth beer of the night. Suddenly, his peace was interrupted by a voice from the living room.

"Harry, how can you watch that garbage? Especially at a time like this! You know how worried I am about that test I've got tomorrow, and all you can do is watch some damn junkie on the tube. Seems like all they do anymore is glorify drug addiction anyway, trying to get you to feel sorry for those bums, just poor, helpless victims of society. Lazy trash is what they really are if you ask me, copping out on drugs all the time. . ."

Harry patiently closed his eyes, taking a long drink from the beer he held in his hand. "Martha, you know Kojak is my favorite show, give me a break, wouldja?"

"Well, I just hate to see drug abuse condoned, that's all. I mean, what effect is this gonna have on the kids anyway?"

"It's just a TV show, Martha. . ."

"Yeah, yeah, I know. Hey, Harry, where's that bottle of Valium I got from Dr. Klein today? I really need a couple if I'm going to get any sleep tonight."

"Haven't you already taken two today?"

"Yeah, but I need a couple more. Two just don't seem to work anymore. Where are they?"

"I think they're in the kitchen. . .hey, bring me another beer while you're up, willya?"

Drugs. In today's world, countless people suffer from unrealistic fear. It's one of the most frequent complaints seen in medical practice, and almost always plays a leading role in psychiatric and behavioral problems. And, clever creatures that we are, we've managed to come up with a variety of ways to lessen anxiety, some good ones, and some not so good. Probably the most common technique is the use of drugs.

When you think of a drug problem existing in our culture, you no doubt get images of heroin, "speed," "acid," "uppers and downers," and skinny, burned-out junkies, much like the scene at the start of this section. But actually, these "illicit" drugs and the people addicted to them account for only a small portion of the drug abuse in our society. The real problem lies with the overuse of the more common, everyday, easily obtained agents such as alcohol, cigarettes, coffee, tranquilizers, painkillers and sleeping pills by common, everyday people just like you and me.

It's a rare bird who's never tried to quell his or her sorrows or unwind with a drink or two. And if used infrequently, there's nothing wrong with this. It's just when we come to rely on this drug to stay calm, to face the world, to keep our anxiety at a bearable level that it stops being social and starts being a real problem. Alcohol is addicting, produces withdrawal effects and damages the body when used to excess whether you're a wino laying in the gutter of skid row, or a corporate executive on Wall Street. Many doctors will tell you that the use or abuse of the "sauce" is associated with a large proportion of the medical problems they see in their everyday work.

Another drug now quickly growing in popularity is Valium (Diazepam), a minor tranquilizer. According to Dr. Blackwell,[4] a medical researcher, Valium is the most widely prescribed drug in the U.S., making up roughly 50 million prescriptions a year. Designed to be used only for a short period of time, Valium reduces feelings of fear and anxiety. When taken correctly, it's a useful drug, and can be quite helpful in making people feel more comfortable in the early stages of therapy or counseling. But it's often abused with people taking doses larger than those recommended by their doctors. When used this way in large amounts and over a long period of time, Valium can be addicting, producing severe withdrawal effects when the person stops taking it. Also Valium becomes extremely dangerous when washed down with large amounts of alcohol, potentially causing loss of consciousness, coma, or possible death.

Avoidance. Another way to cope with unrealistic fears is to avoid the anxiety-producing situations, which we touched on a little in the first chapter. Someone with an elevator phobia, for instance, may cope by simply avoiding elevators and taking the stairs. A fear of flying can be dealt with by taking a bus or train when you want to travel. While sometimes a pain, these don't seriously limit us in pursuing our goals in life.

But how about social fears, or free-floating anxiety? Avoiding others *can* put a damper on our becoming the sort of person we'd like to be. This sort of avoidance ranges from being a social dud or wallflower to extreme isolation. On the short-lived TV series called "All that Glitters," there was one character who, following a divorce, became so fearful of social interactions that he retreated first to his house and then to his kitchen. Finally, his avoidance became so severe, he lived, ate, and slept in the kitchen closet, unable to speak to anyone except his son, and even then, only through the closet door. An extreme example, perhaps, but it illustrates the point we're trying to make.

Social avoidance can evolve into a vicious circle. You stay away from social gatherings because you're afraid of them. Staying away from social contacts makes your social skills more rusty, and the longer you keep this up, the more fearful you'll be to try them out again. You see quickly where this leads you in the long run—nowhere.

We're not talking about this to put down people who use drugs and alcohol to counter this anxiety, or to criticize those who keep to themselves, avoiding facing social fears. The pros and cons of these lines of defense against fear are something you'll have to weigh for yourself, deciding what is right for you. But we would like to point out that there are other ways to cope, ways involving a more active, assertive, positive role on your part, ways more in line with climbing out from under the bridge of fear than with learning to live under it. Because the reality of the situation is that you *can* succeed in beating fear, if you wish to. You can approach your fears directly, actively rather than passively, using the techniques we'll lay out for you in this book. But to do this, you'll have to become aware of just how much you use the methods we've just discussed to cope with your fears, so you can work to reduce them. We'll go into more detail on this later. But first, let's turn back to the subject of fear and its roots— how we learn to be afraid (without really trying).

CHAPTER **THREE**

HOW TO LEARN FEARS (WITHOUT REALLY TRYING)

In the first chapter we saw that fear is a reaction our bodies make to certain things and events, one that gets us ready to fight or run to the best of our ability. But there's another important point to be made about fear: The vast majority of the fears we have, we've learned in one way or another. We weren't born with them.

Nature provides us with only a handful of built-in fears at birth; reactions that occur no matter what, reflexes that happen in virtually all of us. We call these kinds of reactions *unlearned fears* and the situations that cause them *unlearned fear* cues or stimuli. Unlearned fear cues make us aroused, even the first time we experience them—we don't have to learn to fear them. This group of cues includes things like electric shock, extreme heat or cold, loud noises, a sudden loss of support or a fall, and other kinds of physical harm. Even as tiny infants, before we've had a chance to learn much of anything, we fear these types of cues.

As we grow and develop, moving through the world around us, experimenting, touching and being touched, we learn to be wary of other things. Like guns, stern looks from our parents, shady-looking characters on the street, dogs, cats, witches and warlocks, heights, the dark enclosed spaces, water, flying, speaking in public, authority figures, rejection—you name it. These, however, differ quite a bit from the unlearned fears we mentioned above. Because these fears we *learn*. And there're several ways this learning can happen.

LEARNING THROUGH PAIRING[5]

A few years back, John and some friends were cruising the block on Halloween night, talking and laughing, dreaming up daring pranks to wreak upon the neighbors. In the midst of the "battle plan," John spotted a street lamp with its outer globe broken. The huge inner light bulb was exposed.

"Wouldja look at the size of that bulb? I gotta have it."

"Really!" one of the others said. "But how're you going to get it down without getting fried? There's a lot of juice up there, John. . ."

"Aw, it'll be a cinch, man, watch this. . ." John shinnied easily up the slick metal pole, and began to unscrew the bulb. One turn. . .two turns. . .

"AAAArrrggghhh!"

A hot surge of electricity pulsed through his body. He fell trembling to the ground, filled with arousal and anxiety, but otherwise unharmed.

When we contact unlearned fear cues, things associated with them also come to cause a fear response where they didn't before. In John's case, the previously "harmless" bulb and lamppost were paired with the painful shock, and later came to produce a fear response by themselves: They became *learned fear cues*. In the same way, after a person's had a serious car accident, they'll most likely be at least a little afraid of cars and driving, where they once weren't. Someone who's been bitten by a dog may become uptight around dogs; the dogs themselves have acquired learned fearproducing qualities due to their pairings with the unlearned fear cues of the biting.

This diagram shows how John learned to fear lampposts and light bulbs. First, we have the unlearned fear cue of electric shock, which causes anxiety arousal:

electric shock   arousal

But also present at the scene were the light bulb and the lamppost:

light bulb
lamppost
electric shock   arousal

And although they were "neutral" or harmless at first, as a result of this pairing they became capable of causing the same sort of arousal that the shock produced (but now in the absence of shock):

light bulb   arousal
lamppost   arousal

They've become *learned fear cues*.

This type of learning isn't limited just to pairings with unlearned, or harmful stimuli. If a learned fear cue is paired with a neutral one, new learned fear cues will result. To illustrate this concept, let's flash back into the life history of Margie Appleton.

Margie, aged five, somehow locked herself in a closet while playing. Her eyes explored the small, dark area. It was totally black, except for the thin slit of light seeping under the door. They'll be by soon, she thought, any minute now. She listened intently for the slightest sound from the outside world, waiting for what seemed like hours, but could have been only seconds. There were no sounds. She began to worry.

What if they never come? What if I die in here before they find me? What if I use up all the air in here and can't breathe? I'm gonna die in here before someone finds me! Her thoughts raced ahead, imagining the worst things possible. She started to cry out, loudly, banging the door with her small fists.

Her parents found their terrified child a few moments later, after hearing the uproar. They soothed and calmed her, and wondered what it was about the closet that could have scared her so much.

Here we have a child, trapped by accident in a closet—at one time a fairly neutral, harmless situation. While in the small room, she became fearful of never being found, of dying there. She thought and lived some very punishing things. The thoughts (which function as learned fear cues) were paired with the closet, causing this high level of fear arousal. And like the light bulb and lamppost in John's case, the once harmless closet now caused arousal in its own right, through learning. Now, every time Margie finds herself in an enclosed space, the arousal linked with her early bout with the closet returns. The phobia has begun.

So, you see, the cause of unfounded fears lies in unlucky, and often accidental pairings of fear cues with neutral cues. And these quite often involve learned fears to begin with. Actual contact with unlearned fear cues isn't made in many cases. Take a fear of flying, for example. How many people with this fear have actually been hurt in some way related to plane accidents? Not many. But flying in a plane while imagining a crash may result in pairing a lot of fear and anxiety with flying. Result? Planes and flying become capable of causing arousal.

But how can thoughts cause anxiety? How do they become fear cues? Thoughts are, for the most part, verbal—words, things, we say to ourselves. So, one of their functions is that of a cue. And, like any other kind of cue, thoughts can take on a learned fear-producing function as a result of being paired with fear stimuli. Let's take a simple example to illustrate what we mean—the word pain. Pain is often paired with aversive, arousing events throughout our lives, as we

grow and experience events which for the most part are
unlearned fear cues:

    pain

    unlearned fear cue   arousal

  As a result, this word, or thought, comes to cause
arousal on its own, now as a *learned* fear cue:

    pain   arousal

Now, when this type of "loaded" thought is paired with
a once neutral event—such as flying, or sitting in a
dark closet—further learning takes place, resulting in
the neutral stimulus also becoming a learned fear cue:

    pain

    unlearned fear cues   arousal

    pain   arousal

    flying in plane

    pain   arousal

    flying in plane   arousal

So, we have, in essence, a "second order" pairing going
on in this situation, the neutral stimulus taking on fear-
causing properties through pairings with the thoughts,
themselves learned fear cues. This is a simple example,
but you can see how quickly things get complex, each
word and group of words having its own unique history
of pairings within each person.

LEARNING THROUGH WATCHING OTHERS

*The rythmic sounds from the stereo filled the
kindergarten classroom, energizing the smiling
youngsters as only music can, inducing them to dance.
Most of the kids moved in jerky, awkward ways,
sometimes missing the beat of the song, but
nevertheless having a good time.*

  *But not Candy. Candy moved with the disco beat as if
it were a part of her, an internal wave of motion she
rode as easily and effortlessly as a bird floating with
the breeze. Her blonde hair swayed like a fan behind
her as she twirled and stepped with the latest dance
styles. The teacher watched in amazement.*

Later, when Candy's mother came to pick her up after school, the teacher asked where she'd learned to dance like that.

"Oh, her Father and I take disco lessons once a week and practice at home a lot," Candy's mother replied, smiling. "She watches us, and has picked up a lot of moves. She's really quite good, don't you think?"

It's a pretty firmly established fact that we learn a lot of things by just observing others. This kind of learning is called *modeling*. As kids, we learn to talk, to sing, to set the table, to mow the law, to brush our teeth, along with other things too numerous to even try to list by watching good old mom and dad. And learning through modeling keeps up through our entire lives. In fact, there are many things that are much easier to show someone than try to tell them how to do it. Like Candy's dancing.

Along with all the good, useful things we learn by watching others, there's a number of not so useful responses we can pick up this way. Like unrealistic fears.

The hit movie *Jaws* may have created more fear around swimming in the ocean than any other event in history. The great success of the movie centered around its unquestioned ability to produce intense fear in the people who saw it. Watching the hysteria that seized the little east coast resort town in the wake of the series of vicious shark attacks had me, for one, thinking twice about ever taking swims in the sea again. (Not that a fear of sharks is necessarily unrealistic, but a fear of swimming in the ocean probably is.)

And how many youngsters who watch their parents jump with fear when unsuspectingly finding a harmless snake or other reptile in their garden develop that fear themselves? Probably quite a few.

More complex fears may also be picked up through modeling. Social fears, fears of rejection, fears of losing control, and other types may be learned through the modeling of parents or significant figures in our lives.

GENERALIZING LEARNED FEARS[6]

Once we've learned a fear, another process takes place that makes the fear more troublesome. After the affair with the street lamp that fateful Halloween night, John was wary of trying the stunt again. And had the caution stopped there, it wouldn't be a problem. But it didn't.

In a short time, he began showing anxiety around other things as well. Like appliances, outlets, extension cords—in short, nearly everything connected with electricity. Now the fear was a problem, because it interfered with his doing the things he needed to do to get by. It began affecting his day-to-day life.

Likewise, Margie's fear didn't stop with being locked in closets. She became afraid of small rooms, closed-in spaces, and, as we saw, elevators. This shows a very important property of learned fears. Once a situation acquires the power to cause fear, things and events similar to it in some way also come to produce the anxiety. And, this happens even though these situations have never been actually paired with the original fear-producing stimulus. When learned effects spread to stimuli like the stimulus present when the learning took place, we call it stimulus generalization.

Stimulus generalization is probably the main reason learned unrealistic fears persist. Once learned in one situation, the anxiety begins to occur also under conditions *like* the first: John's original fear of light bulbs generalized to *all* electric appliances; Margie's anxiety generalized from locked closets to *all* enclosed, small spaces. A child who's been attacked by a particular dog may then be aroused by *all* dogs, or even all furry, four-legged animals.

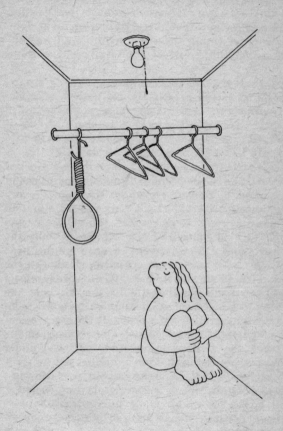

AVOIDANCE AND FEAR[7]

But, if a cue can acquire the powers to cause anxiety by being paired with actual fear cues, won't it lose this power if it's no longer paired with them? If nothing happens to him when John comes in contact with electric appliances, won't they lose their learned ability to cause anxiety? Indeed they will. The trouble is, John won't seek out these objects. And, you won't find Margie hanging around elevators either, the very simple reason being that cues that cause anxiety also cause us to avoid them. So, the person never has the chance to be in the presence of the stimulus when it doesn't lead to harm. Even if it's never again paired with actual harm, the learned cue retains its power to arouse, as a result. The learned anxiety is never *unlearned*. This, then, prevents most fears from going away by themselves. People avoid the learned fear cues, just as they do unlearned ones. And, as long as they're avoided, they retain their fear-producing functions.

So we see a simple but sometimes unfortunate learning pattern. Fear becomes coupled with a cue, an object, scene, or person, as the result of an arousing, aversive experience, or a fear is learned through modeling another. Learned fear cues become ingrained. This fear spreads to other situations like the first, and is then kept alive by the person's avoiding these situations. Avoidance is rewarded because it decreases the anxiety response, but at the same time makes the unlearning of the fear difficult or impossible. The result: the learned fear cues retain their power to cause anxiety and arousal, full-blown, in all their glory.

But there is a key to breaking this pattern: remember that these fears are *learned*. Their causes are many and varied. They involve, as we've seen, unlearned and learned fear cues, along with all sorts of aversive experiences, both real and imagined. Luckily, we don't

ANTHONY J. FEVOLA

really need to know the exact cause of a specific fear or phobia to deal with it. The techniques we discuss later deal more with reducing the anxiety than finding its exact cause. In some cases—like John's—the origin is obvious. In others, it may have been forgotten. In still others, no one knew it in the first place.

The point is that being learned, these fears can be *unlearned*. The presence of unfounded fears doesn't mean you're insane; it simply means you've had some unlucky learning experiences, whether you were aware of them at the time or not. And, some very effective, fairly simple techniques have been found to help you reduce these fears. In the pages that follow, we'll look at how they work.

PART TWO:

Breaking Loose From Unrealistic Fear

CHAPTER **FOUR**

WHERE
DO I
START?

In the first part of this book you were exposed to the various faces of fear. You've seen realistic fear, giving us that extra boost of power when we need it most, helping us break loose from the grips of a crisis or emergency. And you've seen unrealistic fear, the darker side of the coin, with its frequent, unwanted arousal blocking and hampering our attempts at leading a better, more comfortable life. We've looked at the effects of chronic arousal and stress on our health, the wearing down of our bodies and organs, the life-shortening strain of a constant feeling of apprehension and dread. And we've discussed the various ways we tend to cope, the insulation of ourselves from others, the numbing of our bodies through drugs and alcohol, the giving in to the stifling, suffocating cover of fear.

The rest of this book is dedicated toward giving you another option, a more active route, a less harmful way to ward off the churnings and tension we've come to know as fear: a series of self-directed techniques for decreasing your particular fears, whatever they may be.

YOU ARE WHAT YOU FEEL

A large part of the sensation of fear and arousal lies in how we feel, physically. Twisted and taut or loose and languid, tense and uptight or relaxed and calm, muscle tension plays a leading role in this feeling. In Chapter Five you'll find a complete set of exercises aimed at helping you reach a state of deep muscle relaxation, along with step-by-step instructions on how to apply them, when, and how deep muscle relaxation relates to other techniques you'll learn. No matter what kinds of fears you'd like to change, these relaxation exercises will come in handy in helping you combat tension, and aid directly in reducing arousal.

YOU ARE WHAT YOU THINK

Along with how you feel, the sorts of thoughts you have, the way you experience your world, and the kinds of ideas and beliefs you hold about others intimately relate to fear and arousal. Whether you view your world as a negative space, a void brimming with problems you can't solve, people who don't like you, disasters you feel you can't handle, *or* as a positive arena where you can grow, both within yourself and along with your loved ones, a place where problems exist, but so do solutions, where there is hope, where you can learn to overcome the feelings of hopelessness, depresses and alienation that come from fear, can make a great deal of difference in how you handle fear-producing situations as they come up.

We'll present techniques aimed at helping you recognize, actively challenge and modify negative thought patterns and irrational, self-defeating beliefs, enabling you to overcome ways of thinking that add to the development and maintenance of your fear responses.

YOU ARE WHAT YOU DO

Sometimes a cause of uneasiness, especially social fears, relates to your *behavior* in various situations. For instance: Are you one of the many folks who get uptight around people you don't know because you really don't know what to say? Are you uncomfortable trying to make small talk? Do you let pushy or even not-so-pushy people run all over you—even though you hate it—and then put yourself down, feeling like a pushover? Are you afraid to say no? Or yes? Afraid to say "I love you," or even "I like you"?

If you are, you're not alone.

In Chapter Seven, we'll show you how to take a look at what you do, how you do it, what you don't do and how to learn the kinds of social behaviors that'll help you break free from feelings of social awkwardness, buffoonery or cloddishness. In a series of rather simple exercises, you'll learn how to begin, control and end conversations, how to express your real feelings, affections and emotions, how to stand up for your rights as a person and a host of other kinds of social skills. As you progress through these phrases, you'll feel yourself gradually being able to interact with whomever you want, whenever you want, with increased confidence in yourself and your ability to handle social situations.

THE BLENDING OF FEAR

You'll probably find that there's more than one kind of fear behind your discomfort. There might be a combination of fears adding up to form a feeling of uneasiness. For instance, the phobic person might also be bothered by social fears, the socially anxious by phobias and free-floating fear, and so on. So, the techniques we discuss in the chapter on conquering phobias might be useful in helping you deal with a particular social fear that's giving you trouble, like a fear of starting conversations with strangers, perhaps, or of small talk. For the best results with your particular fears, read all the techniques we lay out in the following chapters before starting to use them. This'll help you decide which technique or combination of methods appears to be the best, or the most likely to be effective in helping you.

KEEPING TRACK OF PROGRESS

In each section, we've included charts, forms and other devices you can use to track your progress as you work toward breaking your fears. This step plays a critical role in the technique of self-help, acting as a map, guiding your course, helping you find out whether your fears are changing at the rate and in the way that you want. If you use them accurately, you'll find they can be a big help.

PERSONAL COMMITMENT AND SUCCESS

The approach we're using in this book, as you can see, is a self-directed, self-administered one. We'll cover techniques for decreasing free-floating anxiety, specific phobic fears and social anxieties that actively involve you as the major agent of change, determining the direction things will go. And the responsibility for carrying out the methods we explain, for keeping track of progress, for sticking to the program through thick and thin, is on your shoulders.

We're stressing this seemingly obvious fact for one important reason: When self-directed methods don't work as well as they could, it's nearly always because the person fails to carry them out all the way, applying the techniques carelessly or incompletely, falling victim to the same sort of self-defeatist attitude that serves to maintain fear in the first place. So it's crucial that you follow through with the instructions religiously, even when the chips are down, even when they may make no sense to you, even when they may not seem to be working.

CHAPTER **FIVE**

RELAXATION: INNER PEACE THROUGH MUSCLE TENSION

A veritable mountain of a man, Carl sat nervously in the recliner across from me, staring holes in my desk as his fingers pulled, flicked and picked at every loose thread, spot of lint and microscopic speck of dust within reach of his long arms. His speech quivered as he spoke, a very quiet voice that seemed incongruous with his tremendous size and apparent strength. His face moved with a barely perceptible twitch.

Carl was a very tense person.

Half an hour later, Carl was a different person. He looked almost poured into the recliner, eyes barely slits, nearly asleep, his arms hanging limply on the stuffed chair, a faint trace of a smile on his lips. When he spoke again, it was still rather quiet, but his voice didn't waiver.

"Wow. . .I didn't know that this was what relaxation's all about. . .I've never felt this laid-back in my life."

"You know," he said, looking up across the desk at me, "I guess this's the first time I've every really been relaxed."

We all know what it means to relax. Actually, there are a lot of different kinds of relaxation, different ways of reducing anxiety, each having its own level of tension reduction.

Watching TV, reading a book, daydreaming, going to a movie, plunking out a mellow tune on the old six-string guitar, going for a walk, taking a ride on the bike, lying on a sandy beach, or just sitting on the front porch; all are common ways of reducing the tension that can build up in our bodies after a day of scrambling through a job and the rush-hour traffic on the way home.

But still, how many nights have you lain awake, feeling slightly tense, eyes closed but muscles still taut enough to refuse entry to the calm world of slumber, thinking about what went on that day, what was scheduled for tomorrow, the next day and the day after that, and how in the hell were you ever going to get everything done that you needed to?

Probably *too* many.

In the old days, when times were simpler, tension levels of the average person were no doubt fairly low. But now, things are different. With our increasingly complex life-styles, many new sources of tension have arisen. Traffic congestion, subways, trains, buses, air pollution, noise pollution, water pollution, the evening news reports of sadistic multiple-murders in your neighborhood, the world on the brink of an energy crisis, the cost of food rising and rising and rising. . .

Sometimes the old ways of relaxing just don't work anymore.

Sometimes, no matter how hard we try, we can't get completely relaxed, completely relieved of muscle tension, that queezy stomach, that crick in the back of the neck. In fact, many folks have lived with tension for so long, they just assume that it's a part of life. But this isn't true.

During the 1930s, a type of relaxation technique was developed by a physician by the name of Edmund Jacobson, involving the alternating tensing and relaxing of various muscle groups throughout the body. Later refined and modified by behavior therapists, this method leads to a state characterized by extreme muscle relaxation, along with a nearly complete absence of tension in the body.

The benefits of this kind of relaxation quickly became obvious to the people who used and practiced it. It's been extremely effective in helping relieve the discomfort of fear and anxiety-related problems, as well as grief, anger and similar kinds of difficulties. In fact, deep muscle relaxation seems to be directly antagonistic to emotional arousal, decreasing blood pressure, heart-rate, making us breathe more slowly, combating all the symptoms fear produces in our bodies. The experience it produces is pleasant, restful, calm, soothing, at times nearly meditative in its intensity. And it's rather easy to learn. There's nothing difficult or mysterious about it; you don't have to dress up in exotic robes, surround yourself in flowers, twist your legs in unusual positions, or sit under a pyramid. You can do it lying down, sitting up with your head against the chair, even sitting at your desk, once you get good at it.

And it doesn't take long either. At the beginning you'll need to set aside about thirty to forty-five minutes at least once a day for practicing the technique. Once you master it, it'll only take a few moments to become completely relaxed, and you'll be able to use it nearly any place, any time.

Deep muscle relaxation is one of the primary steps in learning to reduce your fears, regardless of what type or types they may be. So, be sure you follow the instructions to the letter, concentrating on what you're doing, taking plenty of time, in order to learn it well.

It'll come up again and again through the rest of the book to be used in combination with the various procedures described.

Muscle
Relaxation
Exercises

INTRODUCTION

The basic idea of these exercises is to teach you how to relax fully and completely. It has been found that an effective method of achieving relaxation is to tense the various muscles and muscle groups of your body as tightly as you can, holding and studying the tension for a few moments, and then releasing the tension and noticing the difference. The idea is to methodically concentrate on the difference between tension and relaxation. While tensing any specified area of your body the rest of your body should remain as relaxed as possible. As you progress through these exercises, you will learn to enjoy the relaxation more and more as it becomes deeper and more complete. Throughout these exercises, you will notice a series of three dots(...). These dots indicate periods where you are to pause for five or ten seconds and concentrate on the sensations you are feeling at the moment.

GENERAL LOOSENING UP

These exercises are designed to loosen up your major muscles and will take about two or three minutes. Begin by standing up and stretching your hands over your head as high as you can, stretching all of the muscles from your finger tips down to your toes. Hold this tension for a few moments...then relax...Repeat

I'm sorry he can't come to the phone right now...he's practicing his muscle relaxation exercises!

this exercise several times. Now bend forward, tensing the muscles along your back and legs...study the tension for a few moments...then relax and notice the difference...repeat this exercise several times. Next, lightly shake your hands and arms for a few seconds, relaxing all the muscles that you can. Then be seated, preferably in a comfortable, reclined lounge chair, and carry out the following exercises.

RELAXING YOUR HANDS AND ARMS

These exercises will take approximately four to six minutes to complete. You should, at this point, already be seated with both feet comfortably extended out in front of you, your arms and hands resting along the arms of the chair, and your head and neck in a relaxed, resting position. Relax like this for a few moments... now, make your right hand into a tight fist, clench your fist tight—as tightly as you can—and build up the tension in your hand and forearm...study this tension for a few moments...now relax and notice the difference...once more, clench your right fist as tightly as you can, build up the tension, study it...now relax and notice the difference...now clench your left hand and make it into a tight fist. Make the fist tighter and tighter, build up the tension and study it for a few moments...now relax and notice the difference...once more, make your left hand into a tight fist, build up the tension in your hand and forearm tighter and tighter, study this tension for a few moments...and now relax and notice the difference...notice how relaxed your hands are and how much more pleasant the relaxation is compared to tension. Concentrate on relaxing all over for a few moments...next, bend your right elbow, making your right hand into a fist and tensing your forearm and upper arm as tight as you can, build up this tension tighter and tighter, study it for a few moments...now relax...straighten your arm and let the tension flow out...notice the difference between the tension and relaxation...enjoy the relaxation for a few moments...now, once more, bend your right elbow, making your right hand into a fist and building up the tension in your hand, forearm, and upper arm. Build up this tension and study it for a few moments...now relax...straighten out your arm and hand and let all the tension flow out. Concentrate on studying the difference between relaxation and tension...now breathe normally and rest for a few moments...next, bend your left elbow, making your left hand into a fist, and tightly tense your forearm and upper arm, build up the tension in your upper arm, study it...now relax and notice the difference...notice how good the absence of tension feels...enjoy this relaxation for a few moments...now, once again, bend your left elbow very hard, making your left hand into a tight fist and your upper arm muscle into a tight ball, build up the tension as much as you can...study the tension...now relax and notice the difference...let all the tension flow out of your muscles and concentrate on becoming as relaxed as you can...just concentrate on relaxing as completely as you can and remain in this position as the instructions for the next relaxation exercises begin...

RELAXING YOUR NECK, FACE, AND SHOULDERS

These exercises will take about four to six minutes to complete. Take a few moments and continue resting...now let your head roll slowly around for a few turns as loosely as you can...next turn your head to the right as far as you can, building up the tension and studying it...now relax and notice the difference... notice how good the absence of tension feels...now repeat this procedure once more. Turn your head to the right as far as you can, build up the tension and study it for a few moments...now relax and notice the difference...next, turn your head to the left as far as you can...build up tension and study it...now relax, let all the tension flow out and concentrate on studying the difference...once again, turn your head to the left as far as you can, build up the tension, study it...now relax and notice the difference...now bend your head forward, pressing your chin against your chest as tightly as you can, build up the tension...study it...now relax and notice the difference...next, concentrate on relaxing your shoulders. Begin by shrugging or bringing your shoulders up as tightly as you can, build up the tension, study it...now relax and notice the difference...let all the tension flow away...relax all the muscles in your neck and shoulders...relax all over as fully as you can...continue relaxing for a while...

Now concentrate on relaxing your facial muscles. Begin by frowning and furrowing your brow as tightly as you can, build up the tension...study it...now relax and notice the difference...once more, frown and furrow your brow as tightly as you can, build up the tension...study it...now relax and notice the difference... next, move on to your eyes and, closing them, squint them as tightly as you can, build up the tension...study it...now relax and notice the difference...once again, close your eyes and squint them tightly, build up the tension...study it for a few moments...now relax and notice the difference...let all the muscles in your forehead, around your eyes, and all over your face and entire body relax as fully as you can...move on to your lips and tongue. Relax your lips by first pursing them tightly, build up the tension, study it...now release the tension and relax...notice the difference...once more, pucker your lips tight, build up the tension...study it...now relax and notice the difference...now press your tongue against the roof of your mouth, build up the tension and study it for a few moments...now relax and notice the difference...once more, press your tongue tightly up against the roof of your mouth...build up the tension...study it...now, relax and notice the difference . . .notice how much better the relaxation feels in contrast to the tension...now, concentrate on relaxing all the muscles in your neck, shoulders and face...let all the tension flow out...relax deeper and deeper...continue relaxing for a while...

RELAXING YOUR UPPER BACK, CHEST, AND STOMACH

These exercises will last four to six minutes. Keeping the rest of your body relaxed, tense the muscles in your upper back area by raising your shoulders and shrugging them back and up; tense them tight, build up the tension...study it...now relax. Let your shoulders fall down and relax as completely as you can...notice all the tension flowing out of your upper back area...let yourself become more and more relaxed as the relaxation spreads throughout your entire body...now once again, tense the muscles in your upper back area by shrugging your shoulders up and back, build up the tension...study it...now relax, let your shoulders fall, and, as they do, let all the tension flow out of your body...let yourself become more and more relaxed... concentrate on experiencing this relaxation fully... concentrate on reducing even the slightest bit of tension...continue to relax and enjoy this feeling for a few moments.

Now, as you are relaxing, breathe in deeply, filling your lungs as fully as you can and hold it for a moment...exhale, breathe normally a few seconds while concentrating on relaxing more...breathe in deeply and again completely fill your lungs; then hold your breath for a few moments...now exhale and slowly permit the air to leave your lungs, concentrate on experiencing the increasing relaxation as you slowly exhale...breathe normally for a while, letting yourself become more and more relaxed...enjoy this spreading relaxation as you breathe in and out...now once again, breathe in deeply, fill your lungs and hold your breath for a few moments. Study the sensation...now exhale slowly and concentrate on the pleasant experiences as you do...breathe normally again for a while, each time letting yourself become more and more relaxed...once more, breathe in deeply and fill your lungs to capacity; hold your breath for a few moments. Study the tension...now exhale slowly, concentrating on becoming more and more relaxed...let this relaxation spread throughout your entire body...your upper and lower back, shoulders, neck, face, chest and arms are all becoming more and more relaxed as you breathe...as you continue breathing, concentrate on becoming more and more relaxed...

As the relaxation goes deeper and deeper, center your attention on your stomach and abdominal area. Pull in your stomach and make it and your entire abdominal area as tight as you can, build up this tension and study it...now relax and let all the tension flow out of these muscles...notice how relaxed and loose your muscles are...let yourself become more and more relaxed...once again, pull in your stomach and make your abdominal muscles as tight as you can, build up this tension, study it...now release the tension and notice the difference... once more pull in your stomach and make your abdominal muscles as tight as you can. Study this tension for a few moments...now relax, releasing all of the tension in your stomach and abdominal muscles... continue relaxing for a few moments ...next, inhale deeply and, pushing your diaphragm down, extend your stomach and tense your abdominal muscles as tight as you can. Study this tension...now exhale and relax, releasing all the tension from your stomach and abdominal muscles...enjoy this relaxation for a few moments...once more, inhale deeply and pushing your diaphragm down, extend your stomach and tense your abdominal muscles as tightly as you can, study this tension...now exhale and relax, releasing all the tension from your stomach and abdominal muscles... enjoy the ever-decreasing tension...continue breathing in and out for a while, concentrating on becoming more and more relaxed...let all the tension flow out of the muscles in your abdominal area as well as in the rest of your body...as your muscles become more and more relaxed, you feel warm and somewhat sleepy...your eyelids are becoming heavier and it is hard to keep them open.

RELAXING YOUR LOWER BACK, HIPS, THIGHS, AND CALVES

These exercises will last approximately four to six minutes. As your relaxation continues, pay attention next to your lower back. First arch your lower back and tense the muscles there as tightly as you can, build up the tension, study it . . . now, relax and notice the difference. . .concentrate on relaxing your lower back as completely as you can. . .make your entire body more and more relaxed. . .deeper and deeper. . .once again, arch up your lower back and tense the muscles there as tightly as you can, study this tension for a few moments. . .now relax and notice the difference. . .next, tense the muscles in your buttocks, thighs, hips, legs and calves by flexing your buttocks as tightly as you can while at the same time pressing down on the heels of your feet, exerting as much pressure as you can. . . build up this tension...study it...now, relax and notice the difference. . .concentrate on relaxing all of your muscles, deeper and deeper. . .once again flex your buttocks and press down hard on your heels, build up the tension. . .study it. . .now, relax and notice the difference. . .enjoy this relaxation for a few moments. . . next, while resting the heels of your feet, point your toes toward your head and tense all the muscles in your feet, ankles and lower legs, build up this tension. . . study it. . .now relax and once more notice the difference; notice how good the relaxation feels. Once more, point your toes toward your head and tense all of the muscles in your feet, ankles and lower legs. Build up this tension. . .study it. . .now relax and notice the difference. . .notice how soothing the relaxation is. . .let this relaxation spread throughout your body. Enjoy this relaxation for a while. . .

FINAL RELAXATION AND INSTRUCTIONS

Continue to rest and relax as you go through the final set of instructions. These instructions are intended to enhance and intensify the general overall state of deep muscle relaxation already achieved. They will last approximately two to six minutes. By now all of your muscles should be fairly well relaxed. Your eyelids feel heavy, your arms feel heavy and you feel a warm sensation in all parts of your body along with a desire to fall asleep. . .now enhance your relaxation even more by again taking a deep breath, filling your lungs completely and holding this tension for a few moments ...then relax and slowly exhale...notice how relaxing it is as you exhale. . .breathe normally for a while and concentrate on going into a deeper state of relaxation... now once again, breathe in deeply, fill your lungs to maximum capacity, and hold your breath for a few moments. . .study the tension. . .now exhale slowly and notice the increased relaxation as you do so. . .breathe normally for a while and concentrate on eliminating any tension anywhere in your body. . .as you breathe in and out, you will become more and more relaxed. . .the relaxation will go deeper and deeper. . .now once again breathe in deeply and fill your lungs to capacity. . .now hold your breath for a few moments and study the tension. . .now relax and notice the increased relaxation. . .continue breathing normally for a while and, as you do, you become even more and more relaxed. . .deeper and deeper. . .you should now be in a state of complete relaxation. . .enjoy and appreciate the very warm, pleasant, and comfortable experience of complete relaxation.

RELAXATION RECORD FORM

This is a simple device for you to use in keeping a record of your relaxation exercises. This form is useful for a number of reasons. First of all, it serves as a useful reminder for you to practice your exercises. Secondly, it also gives an indication as to the degree of relaxation you have prior to carrying out your training as well as afterwards. This information, in turn, can let you know how well you are succeeding in reducing your anxiety and achieving muscle relaxation.

Please use this form to keep a record of your training in relaxation. Indicate the level of your relaxation before and after each training session by writing in a number in the last two columns on the right from 1 to 5. A score of one indicates that you are anxious, tense or otherwise aroused, while a score of five indicates that you are completely relaxed. In between these two points are scores of two (slightly tense), three (somewhat relaxed) and four (moderately relaxed).

Date and time	Location	Degree of Relaxation Before	After	Practice Time
6/17 5.00 p.m.	At home	1	4	20
6/19 3.30 p.m.	At home	1	4	18
6/20 6.00 p.m.	At home	1	5	22
7/1 8.00 a.m.	At school library	1	4	15
7/3 9.00 a.m.	On commuter train	1	4	10
7/5 5.30 p.m.	At home	1	5	20
7/6 6.00 p.m.	At home	1	5	21
7/10 5.30 p.m.	At home	2	5	10
7/11 4.00 p.m.	At home	2	5	15
7/15 5.00 p.m.	At home	2	5	15
7/17 7.00 p.m.	At home	2	5	20

CHAPTER SIX

CONQUERING FREE-FLOATING FEAR

In the last chapter, we saw how to relax through a series of rather simple exercises, designed to bring about the feelings of peace, ease, comfort and warmth that stem from a complete absence of muscle tension. But while learning and practicing muscle relaxation is a crucial part of our fight against fear and anxiety, there's more to the story.

THOUGHTS AND FEAR

The mind—what we think, feel, say to ourselves, imagine, experience within our private, inner world— plays a tremendously important role in how we feel. Our thoughts and imaginings come to the fore in all the types of fears we've talked about so far, but particularly in the case of general, free-floating anxiety—the kind of vague, nonspecific feeling of uneasiness and tension that plagues so many of us in today's world. Our attitudes about things, the importance we give various people and situations, how we view ourselves and our relations with others, all exert quite an influence on whether we're basically comfortable, positive and happy, or miserable, fear-ridden and unhappy as we move through our lives.

This isn't a new idea. It's been around for a long time, applied for centuries in religion, folk medicine, philosophy and just plain common sense. But for some reason, while we all know that what we think has a lot to do with how we feel, we still let ourselves think in certain patterns, looking at things and situations in ways that foster and facilitate fear, self-depreciation, pessimism and the feeling of helplessness. We allow ourselves to be swept down the river of doubt and discomfort, as if we really couldn't change the way we think even if we *wanted* to, or as if the way we think always reflects *reality,* and if reality's basically dismal and crummy, well, there's nothing we can do about that.

Neither of these are true. We *can* change the way we think, and our thinking *doesn't* always reflect the way things actually are.

POSITIVE THINKING, NEGATIVE THINKING, AND ANXIETY

We've all heard of positive thinking and its power in affecting how we feel and act. There've been countless books written about it, and positive thinking, faith and optimism form the basis for a good many religions. If you think negatively, dwelling endlessly on your faults and weaknesses, you'll tend to feel inadequate, incompetent and anxious. On the other hand, if you concentrate on your strengths and attributes, what you do well, the things you've got, you'll tend to feel more self-assured, comfortable and calm. Independent of the way things actually are.

The fact is, as we saw in Chapter Three on the learning and maintenance of fears, our thoughts act as *cues,* stimuli that can cause fear and tension, or that can make us feel good. And the way we perceive a situation can make all the difference.

Joey Matton is a high school student about to make his first speech before the class. Let's tune in on his thoughts just before the speech:

Well, here I go again. Even though I studied my butt

off the last three days, have all my notes on 5 x 7 cards, typed, numbered and in order in my hand, I'll probably blow it. The class'll think I'm dumb, just like Bobby Jones when he blew it last week. I'll never remember all the things I need to say; I'll be so scared I bet I won't even be able to read these damn cards! After I screw this up, I'll never be able to go back to class....they'll all be thinking about what a jerk I am for messing up this stupid speech. God... I don't feel too good...

All these thoughts, projections, guesses of the way the speech is going to turn out have already stacked the deck against our friend, causing a severe case of the butterflies in the stomach we know as stage fright. In reality, Joey's prepared for the talk, has practiced it, memorizing the material, and nothing *really* stands in the way of it coming off rather well.

Except the negative thoughts going off inside his head, exploding like tiny cannisters of "fear gas" choking him with arousal, increasing the chances that he'll stammer and stumble around because of his nervousness.

Now, let's look at Joey's classmate, Linda Mills, before *her* speech. Linda's done the same amount of preparation as Joey, and the big day's drawing close for her. Her thoughts:

Well, I think all this work is going to pay off. I really know this stuff and I shouldn't have any problem giving the talk. I've got my note cards if I get lost and my conclusions are all organized. I think I did a pretty good job in preparing this material and I'll do a good job giving the speech. I know I will.

While Joey and Linda did the same amount of preparation for the talks, who do you think will present the better speech? And who do you think will be the most relaxed in his delivery? Our money would ride on Linda. In contrast to Joey, Linda's thoughts about the upcoming event are positive, optimistic, self-confident and calmly self-assured. Just as Joey aroused his fear response by thinking negatively, expecting that the worst was going to happen, Linda used her positive thoughts to do exactly the opposite: to calm herself, prepare herself and to boost her confidence in her ability to succeed in the task ahead.

Folks who walk around in a state of arousal tend to talk to themselves in ways that foster this arousal, having negative expectations about the future and about their ability to cope.

If you too, are bothered by pervasive anxiety, the chances are pretty good that negative self-talk may be involved. Examine your own fear responses. How often do you find yourself engaging in negative, apprehensive thinking, resulting in an increase in your fear level? If your answer is, *"more often than I'd like,"* you can use *Technique A* to reverse this kind of thinking.

TECHNIQUE A: POSITIVE THINKING

Step One: Know what situations cause your negative self-talk. Any number of things can trigger negative self-talk. For instance, an unexpected debt may cause negative self-talk about your financial status, or your ability to handle money. In the same way, a vague pain somewhere in your body may cause you to think pessimistically about your health, or lead you to imagine you've got a major illness.

Make a list of things and situations that make you think negatively throughout the day. This will help you identify what conditions cause your negative thinking and give you an idea how often this happens. Knowing what these things are will help you prepare for the next step in combatting negative self-talk.

Step Two: Block the fear response with positive self-talk. When you encounter situations that typically produce negative self-talk, handle them with positive self-talk instead. You've identified most of the things that trigger your negative self-talk. Now, as soon as you come across such a situation, tell yourself positive statements, like:

"I can handle this problem. It's not that important, just take it easy. I must keep calm and relaxed, there's no reason to get uptight. Relax, don't worry, just relax."

Repeat phrases like this to yourself in quick succession immediately on encountering fear-producing situations. By doing this, you can avoid making the negative self-statements, and thereby avoid becoming overly anxious.

To prepare for doing this, it's helpful to go back over the list of things that cause negative self-talk you made in Step One. Consider the list of situations and write down the negative thoughts you typically have in each situation. Now, for each situation, write down several positive thoughts that counter the negative ones. This is good practice for coming up with the positive side of a situation (particularly is you've been looking only at the negative side until now), and also assures that you have plenty of positive statements to use when you encounter the situations. Here's an example of such a list:

SITUATION	NEGATIVE THOUGHTS	POSITIVE THOUGHTS
Business Meetings	I can never come up with good ideas. . . I'm a failure, all my associates probably think I'm incompetent, it's impossible to come up with good ideas. . .	Today, I'll try my hardest to come up with a good idea, but if I don't, it's nothing to fall apart over. . . just relax, and stay calm, and you'll do better than if you're nervous . . . I really am capable of coming up with good ideas if I approach the situation calmly and I'm not incompetent. . .

If you're someone who tends to almost always look at the negative side of things, you may find it hard at first to come up with positive things to tell yourself. But hang in there. The more you do it, the easier it becomes, and you may soon find yourself automatically saying positive things to yourself in situations that used to just cause negative, anxious thoughts.

Step Three: Concentrate on relaxing. While you're telling yourself positive statements, you also need to offset any fear that starts to appear. A good way to do this is to concentrate on complete muscle relaxation (which you learned in Chapter Five) while engaging in the positive self-talk. Make sure you relax as many of your muscles as you can, avoiding clenching your fists and jaws, holding your hands to your face or mouth, or any other tensing that can add to the fear response.

Step Four: Consider productive ways of handling the situation. Now that you've repeated the positive self-talk and relaxed, switch to statements designed to handle and resolve the problem:

"What are my alternatives? I can do this... or this... or this... It seems this alternative is the best, so I'll do it."

While doing this, keep in mind that you'll probably experience a certain amount of anxiety, particularly when you first start to apply these procedures. But as you keep going, stressing the positive and relaxing self-talk, you'll find this small amount of fear will gradually decrease, with a sense of calmness and self-assurance rising in its place.

Step Five: Reward yourself for making positive self-statements. As you go through these steps successfully, reward yourself for doing it. This step is very important in maintaining your following the procedure and in keeping your fear level low. You may want to reward yourself by making the following kinds of self-statements:

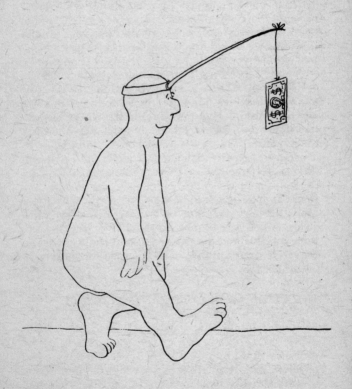

"Congratulations—I really handled that well. I was able to control my fear response! Terrific! I'm proud of myself. It sure feels good to control my own fear and to know I can do it! I know now that what I tell myself affects what I feel, and I can control my fear responses by telling myself positive statements. I really did it!"

You may want to go beyond this kind of self-reward to more elaborate forms, like buying something for yourself after handling several situations well without becoming anxious, treating yourself to a movie, and so on. One of my favorite ways is to literally reach around and pat myself on the back, while telling myself, "Good job, Harold, you really handled that situation well!"

You may be telling yourself, at this point, "This is really simple. There's actually nothing to it." Our answer is that, yes, it is quite simple, and quite effective when carried out properly. But it's always amazed me how many people will try it once or twice and come back to my office saying, "That positive thinking stuff doesn't work. I tried it once last week and I was still anxious!" To repeat a point we made earlier, you've got to apply these procedures religiously, consistently, for them to work. Practice the steps over and over until you more or less automatically make positive self-statements, while rewarding yourself as you do. Only then will the procedures have a solid chance to work, reducing your anxiety and increasing your self-assurance.

IRRATIONAL BELIEFS AND ANXIETY

Along with negative self-statements, there's another form of self-talk that can cause us to be anxious, depressed, or needlessly angry: *irrational beliefs*—attitudes that are basically incorrect, unrealistic and absolute. As a result, they can cause us discomfort and unnecessary arousal. Dr. Albert Ellis, a noted psychologist, feels that irrational beliefs lie at the core of many of the fears and anxieties people have, problems that make their lives less comfortable than they might otherwise be. He's developed a form of therapy, called Rational-Emotive Therapy (or RET), based on the idea that we can actively challenge these incorrect beliefs, replacing them with other, more realistic attitudes when they occur.

IRRATIONAL IDEA #1

The first of Ellis' irrational ideas is that *it is a dire necessity for a person to be loved or approved of by virtually every significant person in his or her community.* Let's look at someone who's had a lot of problems because of this belief.

Sam Fane was a manager at a small firm. A nice, friendly kind of guy, Sam went out of his way to make sure everyone he supervised liked their jobs and him. But as a manager, part of his duties involved checking their work, making sure it was acceptable, complete and appropriately done. Luckily, most of his workers did their work well and rarely needed much watching. But Joe Daniels, a new employee at the firm, was an exception. Joe usually came to work late, snuck out early when he could and generally did his work sloppily. Sam knew this and saw that he'd better get on Joe's case before it got out of hand. So he called Joe into his office.

"How're you doing today, Joe?"

"Terrific, Sam, couldn't be better," Joe said, smiling. "How about you?"

"Fine, just fine. Listen Joe, I've been going over some of your work and —"

"Not bad, eh? I'll tell you one thing, boss, I sure like working here. Everybody's so friendly, and I really couldn't ask for a better supervisor to work for."

"Uh, well, yes. . . I'm glad you like it here." Sam found himself becoming anxious, just as he always did when he had to hand out some criticism to one of his workers.

85

"But about this piece of research. . .couldn't you have done it a little more carefully? I really don't think we can use it the way it is," he said, rather quietly, almost flinching at his own words, though they were anything but harsh.

Joe was silent now, looking at the piece of paper Sam held in his hand, shuffling his feet.

Boy, now I've done it, Sam thought.

"Well, I guess so. . . maybe it is a little skimpy," Joe said, eyes downcast, smile gone.

"Well, maybe a little skimpy, but it's not too bad. I'm just telling you this for future reference. Up to now, your work has been fine," Sam lied. Nearly all of Joe's work had been slipshod and Sam knew it. He just couldn't bring himself to tell this to Joe, not when he looked so hurt by criticism.

"You mean it's just this one piece? Everything else was OK?"

"Uh, yea, it was OK..."

Sam had done it again. It happened whenever he had to give one of his workers some negative feedback—he became very anxious and feared that they'd not like him afterwards. So he wound up burying the criticism so deeply in other things, making it so vague that the person rarely got the point. That's how it went with Joe. Sam had meant to tell him to start coming in on time also, but didn't. So Joe simply went on his way, kept up his below-average work, and Sam had to work extra hard to cover up for it. And Sam ran himself down for this, feeling that he was a bad manager, but he just couldn't bring himself to criticize his people. He had a desperate fear that if he did, he would lose their approval.

Of course, if we think about Ellis' first irrational idea, we see that it's virtually impossible to be approved of by everyone all the time. Striving for this is hopeless and will lead to failure again and again, causing the person who maintains this belief to become anxious and depressed each time he or she has to do something that someone else might not like.

Another, more realistic way of viewing this is to tell yourself:

"It'd be nice if everybody liked me, but that's impossible. I'm bound to do things that others don't like, things that may cause them to disapprove of me. But I don't need to have everyone like me all the time. I can certainly live without it, and it's not the end of the world if I step on someone's toes from time to time."

Ellis' second irrational belief is closely related to the first, and a source of anxiety for many people who hold to it:

IRRATIONAL IDEA #2

You must be thoroughly competent, adequate and achieving in all possible respects in order to consider yourself worthwhile. This idea is as absurd as the first one. It's impossible to be thoroughly competent in everything you do. But people who hold this idea feel worthless, anxious and depressed if they fail at anything.

I once had a client I was training to relax. The first session I went through the series of exercises with her and she seemed to achieve faily deep muscle relaxation. During the second session, I played her a tape with the exercises on it and left the room while the tape was playing, instructing her to simply follow the steps on the tape and relax. Returning later, I found the tape finished and the client lying in a recliner, eyes closed but not looking very relaxed. I asked her to signal me if she wasn't relaxed and told her to take all the time she needed, stressing that there wasn't any pressure on having to relax quickly. All of a sudden, she opened her eyes and began to cry. When I asked her why, she said she felt like a "fool" and "stupid" because she wasn't completely relaxed at the end of the tape. And the more she thought about this, the more tense and anxious she got. She felt worthless, a failure, simply because she was having a hard time relaxing, even going so far as to tell me I probably shouldn't waste my time working with her, because she wasn't worth the effort.

It became pretty obvious that this notion of having to be super-competent at everything to be worthwhile was at work here. I told her that it often took several sessions to learn to relax fully, that trying too hard makes relaxing more difficult and that she certainly wasn't worthless, or a failure just because she was having a hard time relaxing. As we talked about this unrealistic belief, she started to see that it affected many areas of her life. For instance, when her kids acted up, she took it to mean that she wasn't a super-competent mother, and, therefore, she was useless. When her house was messy, she wasn't a thorough housekeeper. Same thing with her job—any mistake, any problem at work made her feel incompetent. So she spent quite a bit of her time thinking about what a useless, worthless failure she was. Result? This lady was depressed and very anxious most of the time, always on the alert to avoid making even the smallest mistake, responding with tension and self put-downs when one happened.

The fact of the matter is that it's *impossible* to be super-competent at everything you do. Sometimes it's hard to be really good at even one thing, let alone everything. All we can do is have a go at it, giving it the best shot we can muster, and leave it at that. Sure, it's nice when we do something well, but it doesn't mean we're worthless if we can't. If we view every failure, every mistake, every slip-up as evidence of a lack of worth, we'll be doomed to a life of frustration, tension, anxiety and self-depreciation.

IRRATIONAL IDEA #3
Certain people are bad, wicked, or villainous, and they

should be severely blamed and punished for this.

Harboring this idea can make you angry most of the time, feeling that folks who're doing something you don't happen to like are wicked animals and should be punished. We all remember many people's reaction to long hair on men during the middle and late sixties: "Those filthy hippies ought to be shot, by God! They're not fit to live in this country!" This belief also forms the basis of bigotry when applied to a whole race or a group of people. You see, thinking this way, can make you walk around angry, accusing and aroused, fists clenched, jaws tight, just because you don't like what somebody is doing. Just as you have the right to do what you want, so do others—even if you don't agree with it.

IRRATIONAL IDEA #4
It is awful and catastrophic when things aren't the way you'd like them to be.

While sitting in my yard one sunny afternoon, I overheard my neighbors talking, and noted this quote: "Oh, my God, it was awful! I'm telling you, it was the worst thing I've ever seen! I don't know how I could stand it!" My curiosity soundly stirred, I couldn't help myself from further eavesdropping. What do you think the speaker was talking about? Being bitten repeatedly by a ten-foot rattler? A house burning to the ground with the family still inside? The speaker's spouse being murdered brutally at the hands of a sadistic maniac?

Actually, the speaker was referring to an incident where the family cat had been chased by a dog, resulting in minor injuries to its tail.

The point is, words like awful and catastrophic are jam-packed with emotion, paired in our minds with things like the bombing of Pearl Harbor, the assassination of a president, or the outbreak of nuclear war. This being so, labelling things this way to ourselves can cause a lot more activation than is usually called for by the situation.

Secondly, if we describe things this way, what'll we feel like if something doesn't work out for us?

"I'll *die* if I don't pass that test!"

"It'll be *all over* if I screw up that speech tomorrow."

"It'll be the *end of the world* if Judy turns down my proposal."

After setting things up this way, we make ourselves very anxious about the event we're thinking about. If it doesn't work out the way we'd like it to, we're bound to be severely disappointed, depressed and even *more* anxious the next time the situation comes up. Ellis calls this kind of self-talk "catastrophizing"—blowing things out of proportion through the use of extreme, emotionally-laden descriptors.

This isn't to say that you shouldn't view things as important, walking through life with an I-don't-care-nothing-really-matters-anyway kind of attitude, because you *do* care, and things *do* matter. It simply means that through the use of catastrophic labels, we can make ourselves needlessly anxious and depressed when things don't go right. He suggests you use milder words, like "unfortunate," or "undesirable." So, if you blow that test, flop in that speech, or suffer some other setback, instead of thinking:

"Well, it's all over now, I'm finished; this is awful!"

try

"Well, it's unfortunate I didn't do better on the test; but next time I'll try harder, and study a bit more in advance. It's not the end of the world and it's an experience I can learn from."

We all suffer misfortune, ranging from flat tires during rush hour to the loss of a loved one—events that may cause a good deal of hurt. But the avoidance of catastrophizing can help in making the burdens easier to bear, allowing us to carry on our lives, to solve the dilemmas that can be solved, and live with the ones that can't.

IRRATIONAL IDEA #5

Human unhappiness is externally caused, and you have little or no ability to control your sorrows and disturbances.

Holding this belief is the same as saying, "I'm at the mercy of outside forces, and there's nothing I can do about anything, so I might as well not even try." As you can probably see, this sort of self-talk leads the way to depression, a helpless floundering avoidance of trying to change the way you feel. You *do* have the power to alter your sorrows, your fears, your difficulties, paving a road to a fuller, more comfortable life.

IRRATIONAL IDEA #6

If something is or may be dangerous or fearsome, you should be terribly concerned about it and keep dwelling on the possibility of its occurring.

An example of this sort of self-talk might be the person who is constantly anxious over the possibility of nuclear attack. Sure, it's possible, and it would certainly be fearsome if it did occur, but to dwell on the possibility all the time serves only to mobilize anxiety and fear and gets in the way of other, more productive types of activity.

IRRATIONAL IDEA #7

It's easier to avoid than to face certain life difficulties and self-responsibilities.

In many ways, this is similar to the ostrich who sticks its head in the sand when faced with danger, feeling that it's safe because it can't see its enemies. Everyone but the bird knows that this is a lot of seed.

It's nearly always better, both in the short run and the long, to face your difficulties head-on. That's the only way you're ever going to figure out how to solve them. Avoidance, denial of obvious problems accomplishes nothing, and the problems often get worse over time, becoming harder and harder to handle. Sticking your head in the sand won't make the problems and responsibilities go away. It just puts temporary blinders on you to hide behind while the problems grow worse.

IRRATIONAL IDEA #8
You should be dependent on others, and you need someone stronger than you to rely on.

This too, is a cop-out type of philosophy. It fosters a passive, submissive, non-assertive approach to life's problems and difficulties, rather than a direct, self-reliant, active mode of dealing with life. We don't need someone to depend on, someone to call the shots for us. If we're ever going to reach our goals, reach out and seek the many wonderful experiences and rewards life has to offer, we've got to believe that we are strong enough to call our own shots.

IRRATIONAL IDEA #9
Your past history is an all-important cause of your present behavior, and because something once strongly affected your life, it should indefinitely have a similar effect.

Irrational Idea #9 probably has its root in the traditional psychoanalytic movement in psychology. Simply put, one of the postulates of this theory is that traumatic experiences, particularly with regard to sex, toilet-training and our parents, have strong, nearly irreversible effects on our "personality structure," especially in the dynamics of our "unconscious." The unconscious is the area of our minds that shuts off to us the parts we're not aware of, but which still controls our actions—the hidden inner realm of ourselves to which entry is forbidden. Since we can't (according to this notion) change our early experiences and their effects on our personality, we remain mere slaves to this darker side, forever pawns to our own development, helpless players in the game of our own lives, to be pushed and pulled, this way and that, by forces beyond our control to modify or alter.

Early experiences do, in fact, have an effect on us and on our behavior, as do current experiences, traumatic and not so traumatic. They cause us to be happy, sad, anxious, depressed, elated and can go a long way in determining how we feel and respond with regard to many things. But the point to remember is that while past history is certainly an influence on us, *we can change the way we are.* We can overcome unfortunate experiences, hurtful memories, major failures and serious losses. We're not slaves to our past history. Just because something once happened, or affected our lives doesn't mean it'll always do so. That is, unless we let it by giving in to this pessimistic philosophy, by allowing ourselves to be helpless in the face of our experiences.

Our personalities are really nothing more than what we think, what we feel, what we do. Just as we can change these things (which we certainly can, by using techniques like you're seeing in this book), we *can change,* essentially, our personalities. Irrational Idea #9 is yet another belief that can, if we allow it, keep us rooted to the *status quo,* stagnant with our fears and anxiety, preventing us from trying to change, from trying to make our lives better, more comfortable, happy ones.

IRRATIONAL IDEA #10
You should become quite upset over other people's problems and disturbances.

We've all known folks whose main purpose in life seemed to be to watch over all the other people in the world, folks who spent the large part of their time fretting over the problems of their friends, relatives, acquaintances, even people in the newspapers who've suffered the winds of ill-fortune. With all the tragedy and despair that comes at us from all sides these days, the headlines in the papers, the horror stories on the news each night, we're exposed to the problems of others constantly. And an over concern with it all can easily lead us to an "Oh-my-God-what's-going-to-happen-next" consciousness, if we let ourselves get carried away.

But don't get us wrong. Concern, sympathy, empathy and help to our friends' and loved ones in distress is a natural response, one that is a big part of what makes us human. But an overreaction, a preoccupation with other's problems, can only lead to a spinning of our wheels and to our becoming so upset we can't really do much to help anyway.

IRRATIONAL IDEA #11
There is invariably a right, precise and perfect solution to human problems, and it's catastrophic if this correct solution isn't found.

This idea is closely akin to idea #4. When faced with a problem, a person having this belief will rack his or her brain, searching over and over for the perfect solution. The usual result is frustration, anger and depression when all the solutions found seem to be just this side of ideal, each having some flaw or other in it. And, having failed to find the Perfect Solution, the person will go on to catastrophize about it.

The point is, there probably isn't ever a perfect solution to a given problem—just those that are better than others. So, the only thing you can do is pick the best out of the ones you've come up with and go with it, rather than spending all your time fretting, sweating and getting upset because of the slight flaws it may have.

Now, how do we challenge these beliefs when they crop up and cause problems?

TECHNIQUE B: COMBATTING IRRATIONAL BELIEFS
Step One: Identify your irrational beliefs. Do you

hold any of the irrational beliefs we've discussed here?
Chances are, if you're like the rest of us, you do. The
first step in disputing these attitudes is to identify
them. Below, we have included a form you can use to
write them down as they come up. Each time you find
yourself becoming overly upset, think of these
attitudes, and see if there's one that's operating to
facilitate this feeling. When you find it, write it down.
Step Two: Dispute the irrational beliefs. For each
irrational belief you identify, write down a rational,
more realistic statement you can use to counter it on the
Changing Beliefs Form. Think of as many ways to
dispute the irrational belief as you can, because the
more you have, the easier it'll be to counter the idea
when it occurs.

For example:

Changing Beliefs

Irrational Belief	*Rational Statement*
1. Everyone must like me.	1. Everyone doesn't need to like me since it is impossible to accomplish. I know that I don't need to have everyone like me.
2. I always have to be right.	2. I don't have to be correct always. While I may strive for this goal, it's not a major failure if I fail to achieve it. It's *impossible* to always be right.
3. No one should ever get mad at me.	3. People *will* get mad at me, and sometimes they'll be justified in having anger toward me and other times they won't. I can accept anger from others without crawling like a worthless slob.
4. I should never get mad.	4. It's human to get mad and I'm human so I will get mad from time to time. It's not an unforgivable sin to get mad.

Provided next is a blank form for you to list your irrational beliefs. After you list these irrational beliefs, practice reciting the corresponding rational statement until you are able to easily recite it when you encounter situations which previously evoked the irrational statement.

Changing Beliefs	
Irrational Belief	Rational Statement

Step Three: Evaluate how well your disputes are working. As you progress with countering your irrational beliefs, assess the effects on your feelings and mood. Do you feel calmer? Less anxious? Do you find yourself returning to "normal" much sooner after an upset than you did before you began this technique? If not, you're probably letting too many instances of the beliefs slide by, or you're not convincing yourself with the disputes. This procedure, like Technique A for changing negative self-talk, requires constant, consistent application to be effective. So if it doesn't appear to be working as well as you'd like, hang in there and try harder.

Step Four: Reward yourself for disputing irrational beliefs. As you find yourself getting more effective at disputing your irrational beliefs, reward yourself for your progress. As we mentioned earlier, self-reward is an important step in maintaining self-produced changes in behavior, so use it lavishly. Don't skimp on self-rewarding—go out and treat yourself to something you really enjoy.

REALISTIC EMOTION AND EMOTIONAL OVER-REACTIONS

After reading these beliefs, you might be thinking: "But if I get rid of all these attitudes won't I be just an uncaring, emotionless, mechanical blob, going through life denying my feelings, not giving a damn about others, or myself? I'd rather have emotions that become uncomfortable at times than none at all!"

Technique B isn't aimed at eliminating your emotions. Far from it, actually. In the person bothered by pervasive anxiety, depression, or anger, the problem isn't the emotion. It's the extent to which the emotion *affects what they do.* Anger, hurt, sadness, depression, fear—all are very human, very natural, very normal reactions to certain kinds of events in our lives, just as happiness, elation, joy and love are. To not be able to feel these emotions would be a shame. It'd rob the person of many of the experiences that add to the fullness, the intensity, the uniqueness of our lives.

But how about the person who's nearly *always* anxious? Almost *always* depressed? *Always* angry? Ellis' techniques aim toward avoiding overreactions and emotional extremes that get in the way of our happiness, our growth, our development as people. Someone losing his or her spouse to death or divorce may well be depressed for a while. But holing up in the house for weeks or months at a time, crying and catastrophizing, refusing to see others, would suggest an overreaction, something that's getting in the way of the person carrying on with his or her life, interfering with overcoming the loss.

Actually, many of us don't need something as bad as that to send us into orbit. Simple things may cause us to overreact, like the dishes not being done, the dog barking, the boss not liking the new project we've written up, our friend passing us in the street without saying "hello," in short, the host of things that go wrong in the course of our traveling through life. And if we let ourselves get aroused over things like this, we're going to plagued with an uncomfortable kind of emotionality, a kind that's not a prerequisite for being human.

That's where these techniques come in handy: in helping us handle the everyday (and not so everyday) sorts of upsets that can, if we let them, keep us in a more or less constant state of tension, depression, or anger because of the way we look at them.

And that's *not* robbing you of your emotions. It's giving you a hand in viewing the things going on around you in some sort of perspective, within a framework that'll help you actively overcome setbacks and problems, rather than spinning your wheels in the mud of emotional overreaction.

That, my friend, is a useful skill to have.

TECHNIQUE C: BEATING ANXIETY BY SLOWING DOWN

The morning was sunny and warm, clouds drifting lazily across the sky, as I drove along the highway toward the Gulf Coast bound for the beach. I looked to the side of the road and saw a large, new sign reading: SLOWING DOWN MAY JUST SAVE YOUR LIFE!

I laughed to myself as I considered how true this was in many ways. I've seen so many people in my practice who've never really learned to slow down, to lower the hectic pace they keep up in their lives. Seemingly in perpetual motion, these folks go through life as if it were a race, a golden decathalon with tracks paved with dollar bills, contracts, stocks, bonds, awards and all the other symbols of success in our culture.

The curious thing about many of these people is that *they* often don't feel they're rushing at all. To many of them, working twelve to fourteen hours a day, six to seven days a week, is a perfectly normal pace. Why, doesn't everyone work at this rate?

Nor do they even suspect that their hectic lifestyles might be related to the complaints they come in to see me about: their fatigue, nervous tension, listlessness, insomnia and vague aches and pains.

Some don't get the message until they feel those first sharp, paralyzing pains of a heart attack ripping through their chest, or the searing, burning feeling of a peptic ulcer. Only then, it may already be too late.

Not that everybody should quit work and lay around all day watching soapies and game shows in the interest of their health. But there *is* a happy medium, a comfortable midpoint, somewhere between inactivity and the continual, nonstop striving to get that bigger house, that fancier car, that better job, that fatter bankbook. This middleground is perhaps what we should be looking for.

But how do we slow down? How do we slacken the pace, without losing ground; ease up a little, while still going for the things we want out of life? Here're a few steps for helping you ease some of the tension in your life caused by too fast a pace.

Step One: Determine your priorities. The process of winding down begins with a thoughtful contemplation of what's really important in your life, and how important these things are relative to others. While you probably already have an idea of what you priorities are, it's helpful to make these explicit, laying them out on paper, to see if you may be spending a lot of time chasing a carrot that's really less important than those things you're giving up for the chase.

For instance, making money and being a success at what you do are nice goals, desirable, healthy and common to nearly everyone. But what about those who spend so much of their time pursuing these goals that they never get to see their spouses or kids? Or their friends? Is making money and being a success more important, higher on their list of priorities than being a good parent, or a good spouse? Is it more important than developing and maintaining lasting and meaningful friendships? If so, then they're doing it right; if not, they need to change their schedules.

To help you evaluate your priorities, here's a sample test, covering various life areas.

My List of Priorities:
What's Really Important

1	2, 3, 4, 5	6, 7, 8, 9, 10
Not Important At All	Of Average Importance	Of Great Importance

You are to rank each of the following goals on this scale from 1 to 10 so that you can see what is and is not really important to you.

1. Being a good parent.   1 2 3 4 5 6 7 8 9 10

2. Spending more time with children.   1 2 3 4 5 6 7 8 9 10

3. Spending more time with my spouse.   1 2 3 4 5 6 7 8 9 10

4. Being a success.   1 2 3 4 5 6 7 8 9 10

5. Making money.   1 2 3 4 5 6 7 8 9 10

6. Doing more family activities.   1 2 3 4 5 6 7 8 9 10

7. Spending time alone.   1 2 3 4 5 6 7 8 9 10

8. Being with friends.   1 2 3 4 5 6 7 8 9 10

9. Social activity (parties, etc.)   1 2 3 4 5 6 7 8 9 10

10. Advancing in my job.   1 2 3 4 5 6 7 8 9 10

11. Helping others.   1 2 3 4 5 6 7 8 9 10

12. Having more free time.   1 2 3 4 5 6 7 8 9 10

The above are just a few of the desires people have. Add all of your additional goals or desires on the lines provided, and rank them from one to ten.

_____

_____

_____

_____

_____

Now, after you have ranked your goals or desires, list all of those that are an 8, 9, or 10, starting with the highest. Rank these desires in order of the strongest, followed by the next strongest and so forth.

_____

_____

_____

_____

_____

_____

_____

_____

_____

After you've ranked these goals, put a checkmark next to each one that's in conflict with another. Now, look at the conflicting desires and decide which of the two is more important. To *you*.

Once you've figured out and ranked your important goals, start changing your schedule to fit these priorities, bringing your behavior in line with your wants and desires.

Many folks find by going through this little exercise, that the things causing the greatest stress, the most tension in their lives, aren't necessarily the ones that're most important to them.

How about you?

Step Two: Relax through "braking." We all know what the word "braking" means: to apply one thing to slow the momentum of another. Like when the brake pads are applied to the wheels of your car to slow them down. Well, in our use of the term here, we're talking about you applying your willpower and self-control to slow down *your* momentum.

Free time during the day. Schedule five-ten minutes of "brake" time about four or five times each day. During these periods, put your feet up and relax, using the exercises we showed you in Chapter Five. Concentrate on the soothing feelings of relaxation, while at the same time letting thoughts about work and problems flow gently from your mind. Don't try to push them away, but just allow them to slowly dissipate, dissolve and fall from your consciousness.

Daydreaming. During these braking sessions, let your mind drift toward peaceful thoughts and imagery. Imagine scenes that you find relaxing and put yourself there, *in your mind.* One of my favorites is to imagine myself floating on an air mattress on a calm lake, gazing lazily up at the clouds as they move slowly through the blue sky, enjoying the feelings of silent weightlessness, calm, warm breezes wafting across the water, and the sensations of the gentle movement of

Fred, you've got to quit storing up your emotions like this!

waves beneath my raft.

Or lying in a field of tall grass, feeling the coolness of the long blades against my body, as I hear the wind blowing softly through the trees, the slight, hypnotic music of birds coming and going with the breeze, the sound of the leaves as they float from the branches in their journey toward the earth.

Make up your own daydreams, using whatever images make you feel relaxed, content, peaceful. (Rolling in a pile of 100 dollar bills?) Sexual fantasies are often relaxing, too, and can usually take your mind far away from your work, depending on how good you are at imagining.

The more you do this, the better you'll get at it, and the deeper your relaxation will be during these breaks. You'll find yourself returning to the rigors of work feeling relaxed, renewed and ready to dive in again more calmly and comfortably.

Step Three: Get away as often as you can. The ultimate in breaks, of course, is getting away altogether, be it for a few hours, days or weeks. Take advantage of your free time by actively engaging in recreational activities, hobbies, sports, exercising, outings, anything that tends to relax you.

While getting away, don't forget to leave your stressors behind. Leave your briefcase at the office, along with the other things that trigger your stress responses. And forget about work. Use the imaginery techniques we just talked about if you feel yourself becoming preoccupied with work-related stressors.

Above all, arrange these longer breaks for having fun. I've seen folks come back from lengthy vacations feeling more tense and harried than when they left because of all the hustling and bustling they went through cramming everything in that they wanted to do. Don't hurry, plan your vacations leaving plenty of time for just plain relaxing.

CHAPTER **SEVEN**

FREEING YOURSELF OF PHOBIC FEAR

Carolyn Rhinehart strolled easily down the busy sidewalk, enjoying the pleasant weather, the light breeze on her face and the fact that it was Friday. She looked forward to the weekend coming up; she and her roommate Suzy had plans to go to the beach and just relax, basking in all that lazy sunshine.

I can't wait to just lie there and do absolutely nothing, she thought, smiling to herself. She'd had an unusually busy week, with the boss on vacation and many of the other employees having days off, taking advantage of the warm days and balmy nights of early summer.

In the middle of thinking about how good her boyfriend, John, was going to look in that new bathing suit she'd bought for him, she abruptly stopped walking and gasped.

Coming down the sidewalk straight at her, was a stubby, shabby little man, walking a stubbier, shabbier little dog. To an observer, the sight would've probably been comical; except for the clothes on the man, and their sizes, the dog was nearly identical in appearance *to its owner. But Carolyn missed the humor.*

She stood paralyzed, trembling, heart thumping, literally cold with fear, a fear that was growing stronger with each step the man and his dog took toward her.

She finally let out a shrill shriek and bolted, running crazily across the street amidst a flurry of blaring horns, screeching tires, and cursing drivers.

The man and his dog looked after her, both with puzzled expressions across their muzzles, shaking their heads together in wonderment.

A block away she stopped and leaned against a lamppost, trying to calm herself. This is getting a little ridiculous, she thought, I must've looked like a veritable madwoman, running from that sorry little dog. She reddened with the thought. Suzy's right. I've got to do something about this. I could've been killed, running into the traffic like that. I'd better go see that therapist before something really dumb happens.

When Carolyn first came in to see me, she was a little embarrassed over her intense fear of dogs. Although she knew rationally that the vast majority of dogs she typically came across wouldn't hurt her, she simply couldn't help herself. They scared her to death. Just talking about them made her noticeably anxious.

"I really do feel silly," she said, looking down at her clenched hands.

"Well, there's really no need to, Carolyn. You're not alone in your fear of those furry little critters, that's for sure. It's a relatively common phobia. "In fact," I smiled, "I once treated a guy who looked like a fullback for the Dallas Cowboys for a fear of dogs. He got over it."

"Really?" She looked up, hope glistening in her eyes.

"Really. There's a fairly simple procedure for helping you overcome irrational fears, one that works amazingly well in most cases. It's called systematic desensitization."

SYSTEMATIC DESENSITIZATION[10]

Systematic desensitization—a lengthy, complicated name for a rather simple technique developed by Dr. Joseph Wolpe in the mid-fifties as a way of helping people overcome phobic fears.[11] Basically, systematic desensitization (or *SD*, for short) involves replacing the fear response to a phobic stimulus with a relaxation response. In other words, you'll work toward getting rid of your fear by learning to relax instead. This involves a three-step process: building anxiety-stimulus hierarchies, deep muscle relaxation and visualizing scenes from your hierarchy while deeply relaxed.

In the pages that follow, we'll discuss these three steps in detail, including instructions, exercises, and hints to help you carry them out. But, before we study them, let's take a brief look at each of the steps to give you an overview of what we'll be doing.

Building Anxiety-stimulus Hierarchies. SD exposes a relaxed person to a graded series of imagined scenes relating to their specific fear. You imagine yourself in a variety of aversive situations while trying to remain as relaxed as you can. Generally, you do this step by step. You begin with scenes causing little or no anxiety, gradually moving toward those scenes holding the most fear, rather than jumping into the worst scene you can imagine, right away. We call this ordered series of scenes an anxiety-stimulus hierarchy.

You'll design your own personal hierarchies—as they apply to whatever fears *you* have—ranking and ordering the scenes as you prepare for the actual desensitization process.

Deep Muscle Relaxation. As we described in Chapter Five, this type of relaxation plays a major role in SD. So make sure you've learned how to achieve this state, through the exercises we've laid out, before trying to go through the steps in SD.

Visualizing The Hierarchy Scenes. You'll be ready to begin the actual desensitization process once you've built the hierarchies for your fears and learned to relax deeply. This involves replacing your anxiety to scenes, with relaxation.

First, you must relax *completely*. Once there, you'll begin imagining the first scene of you hierarchy, while enjoying the rewarding relaxed state. If no anxiety occurs, you'll move on to the next scene and visualize it, again concentrating on remaining totally relaxed.

If at any time you feel anxious, you'll be instructed to stop thinking about the scene and relax deeply again. Once you achieve this, you'll try again to imagine the scene without fear-arousal.

In this way you'll proceed through the entire hierarchy until you can imagine all the scenes without anxiety. This may take anywhere from ten to fifteen or more "sessions," depending on, among other things, how intense the fear is, how well you've designed your list and how clearly you're "seeing" the scenes.

A NOTE ON VISUALIZING

The ability to imagine the specific scenes clearly and easily is important for this technique to work. It's based on the notion that you react to imagined scenes in much the same way that you react to real-life events. Many of you will find you can imagine or "see" things pretty easily. But those who can't do this right off, can develop it with practice. Before beginning self-directed SD, you should check yourself out to see how well and how quickly you can bring, hold and "stop" images and scenes. If you can imagine scenes rapidly and clearly, as well as stop them under your own control, this part of the process shouldn't cause any problems. But, if you do have trouble, take time out and practice using the following steps.

First, sit in a chair, in any room in your house, and look around for a few minutes. Then, close your eyes and try to "recall" the image of the room, going through all the details in your mind—the color of the walls,

111

carpet and ceiling, the furniture, the types of plants, wall decorations, and so on—until you can actually "see" the room in your mind. Once you can do this, try it in another room.

Now, pick up a novel and read a page containing some kind of action. After you read it, close your eyes and again visually imagine in your mind what took place in the passage you just read. Pay close attention to details, appearances, even smells and feelings if you can. Repeat this over and over with different scenes until you can conjure up the situation in your imagination as clearly and vividly as if it were actually happening. Once you can do this, you'll be in good shape for the visualization step in SD.

Now that we've run through the bases of SD, let's prepare to start the real thing.

ANXIETY-STIMULUS HIERARCHIES: WHAT THEY ARE AND HOW TO BUILD THEM

TYPES OF HIERARCHIES

As we've said, anxiety-stimulus hierarchies are lists of scenes that involve events related to your specific fears. They begin with scenes causing little or no anxiety and progress to those causing a great deal of anxiety. In this section, we'll look at some of the distinct types of hierarchy designs, followed by step-by-step instructions for developing your own.

Most hierarchies fall into two classes: those involving *distance* in time or space from a feared object or event and those involving a specific *theme* the anxiety focuses around.

Distance Hierarchies

One of the most common ways of listing fear scenes is to rank them according to distance in space or time from the phobic object. For instance, a hierarchy for a spider phobia may begin with a scene placing the person far from the insect. From there the scenes gradually bring the spider closer and closer, until it actually touches the person. In the same way, a hierarchy for a fear of exams may begin with someone thinking about a test a month away and end with thinking about actually *taking* the exam.

A good example of a distance hierarchy is the following one for a fear of looking out a window of a tall building.

1. *Walking onto the first floor of a tall building.*
2. *Going to the window on the second floor and looking out.*
3. *Looking out of the window from the third floor.*
4. *Looking out of the window from the fourth floor.*
5. *Looking out of the window from the fifth floor.*
6. *Looking out of the window from the sixth floor.*
7. *Looking out of the window from the seventh floor.*
8. *Looking out of the window from the eighth floor.*
9. *Looking out of the window from the ninth floor.*
10. *Looking out of the window from the tenth floor.*
11. *Looking out of the window from the eleventh floor.*
12. *Looking out of the window from the twelfth floor.*
13. *Looking out of the window from the thirteenth floor.*
14. *Looking out of the window from the fourteenth floor.*
15. *Looking out of the window from the fifteenth floor.*
16. *Looking out of the window from the sixteenth floor.*
17. *Looking out of the window from the seventeenth floor.*
18. *Looking out of the window from the top floor.*
19. *Being on the top floor, window open, leaning over and looking out.*

Theme-Oriented Hierarchies

This type of sequence involves changing different

113

parts of the theme of situation which causes the anxiety, beginning with points that cause little fear, and moving to those producing the most anxiety. Think of a hierarchy for the fear of public speaking, for instance. The type of audience present, as well as its size, has a lot to do with the amount of fear produced, in this kind of phobia. So, the "quality" or type of people present in the scenes may begin with children or close friends, moving to other kinds of people, then perhaps to a group of professionals in the area the person is speaking about. Another example is the following hierarchy for a fear of being watched, in which the number and kinds of people watching the person vary throughout the scenes.

1. *Walking outside of your house and saying hello to your neighbors.*
2. *Walking down the street and exchanging greetings with the postman.*
3. *As you walk by a large crowd of people waiting for a bus, you trip and they stare at you.*
4. *As you walk into a crowded supermarket, you notice that the people waiting to be checked out are staring at you.*
5. *In the supermarket as you're trying to pull out a grocery cart that's stuck, everyone is watching you.*
6. *You drop a large jar of pickles, and everyone in the store stares at you.*
7. *Walking into a large crowded department store, you drop your coat and all of the other people in the store stare at you.*
8. *When you're checking out in a crowded line, the clerk overcharges you. You bring this to his attention as the crowded line watches.*
9. *You're at work and several fellow workers standing behind you are watching you work.*
10. *Your boss joins a gathering of fellow workers and they're all watching you work.*

11. *You make a mistake at work, with your boss bringing it to your attention. There is a crowd of fellow employees looking on and they're laughing.*

Mixed Hierarchies

Hierarchies often combine distance *and* theme-oriented items. These "mixed" hierarchies may be the most frequent type, perhaps because they're flexible in showing different dimensions of the particular fear involved. Consider the following fear of dentists hierarchy, for example.

1. *You're on the way to the dentist's office.*
2. *You walk into the dentist's office.*
3. *You're seated in the dentist's waiting room and waiting your turn.*
4. *Your dentist walks by and says, "Hello."*
5. *You get up and walk into the dentist's examining room and are seated.*
6. *The dentist looks into your mouth.*
7. *The dentist checks all of your teeth.*
8. *The dentist starts probing your teeth with a hand instrument.*
9. *The dentist begins scaling your teeth with a hand instrument.*
10. *The dentist begins to clean your teeth.*
11. *The dentist bears down hard and your gums begin to bleed a little.*
12. *Your gums bleed more as the dentist continues to clean your teeth.*
13. *The dentist starts probing teeth for a soft spot.*
14. *She finds a soft spot and begins to probe deeper.*
15. *The dentist then uses the electric drill to bore out a soft spot in your tooth.*
16. *Drilling continues.*
17. *She has finished drilling your tooth and then cleans out your mouth and begins to fill your cavity.*

18. *She locates a decayed tooth and tells you that she's going to extract it.*
19. *The dentist begins to extract your tooth.*
20. *You have a great deal of difficulty and discomfort as she extracts your tooth.*

The first items deal mostly with distance, in terms of time away from the appointment, while the latter ones involve theme items, describing the dentist's actions and the person's reactions to them.

In truth, almost as many types of hierarchies exist as there are fears. Each one has to be custom fitted to the person and fears involved. We've included several sample hierarchies for you to look over in Appendix 1. They involve many fears and include the types of items we just discussed. Read these over once or twice to get familiar with them before you begin to build your own list. You may well find one that relates to your specific fear. If so use it as a model for your own hierarchy.

STEPS IN WRITING YOUR OWN HIERARCHIES

Now that you've read about some of the different types of hierarchies and looked at several examples, you should have some idea as to what's involved in writing them.

First, write your irrational fears down on a piece of paper. Look at the list and see if some resemble others, like a fear of crowds and a fear of public speaking. A group of similar specific fears may, in truth, be the result of a single larger fear. For instance, the two fears we just mentioned could be related to a more general fear of being in a large group of people. If so, we can design a single hierarchy involving the larger fear rather than two lists relating to the specific fears.

Having chosen your fears and grouped them together, pick the one that's causing you the most trouble right now. If you're a salesperson with a fear of meeting new people, for instance, this is probably the one you'll want to work with first. Now with pencil, paper and fear in hand, do the following:

Step One: Describe The Fear. Write a brief description of the specific problem you're going to work with at the top of a blank sheet of paper.

Step Two: List Fear-producing Scenes. List all the situations relating to your fear that cause arousal. Let's use a fear of electricity as an example. Some scenes would involve turning on electrical appliances, or, even more aversive, plugging a cord into an electrical outlet. Receiving a small shock would be extremely fear-producing.

Make sure to describe the scenes clearly and in detail in this step. Later on, you'll imagine the scenes, and it's important to be able to do this easily. The more detailed and vivid you make your scenes, the better you'll be able to visualize them later.

Don't leave out any that you can think of. If you feel later you have too many scenes to work with, you can delete some then. But for now, try and get all of those you can think of down on paper.

Step Three: Rank The Scenes. Once you've listed all the possible conditions linked with your fear, you'll need to rank and order them according to how anxious they make you. A good way to do this is to assign "subjective units of disturbance" (*or suds*) to each scene. In this technique (developed by Wolpe and Lazarus, 1966) you give each scene a score value, ranging from 0 to 100 suds. A score of 0 suds refers to *no* anxiety being produced, while 100 suds means imagining the scene causes *extreme* arousal.

So, for an electricity phobia, sitting and listening to a radio would probably be close to 0 suds. Plugging in a radio may be rated as high as 75 to 80 suds, while receiving a small shock might be scored 100 suds.

Using the suds technique, assign a value to each of the scenes you listed in Step Two. After you finish this, take another sheet of paper and relist the scenes in

117

order of their suds value. Begin with the lowest score and proceed to the highest scene. You've now got your first rough anxiety-stimulus hierarchy.

Step Four: Put On The Finishing Touches. Now, smooth out your hierarchy and put on the finishing touches. You should have roughly the same suds difference between all the scenes in the hierarchy for the best results. In other words, don't have a scene fairly low in suds followed by one that's high. A good difference to have between scenes at the beginning of the sequence is about 10 suds. Toward the end, when the scenes are more disrupting, it may be best to have smaller differences between items (5 suds or less). If you have a large gap in suds between items, design scenes that will fit in that space and add them to your hierarchy.

You may have any number of scenes in your finished hierarchy. But, a list that's too long may be pretty hard to work with. Most often, a hierarchy has 10 to 20 scenes in it, 20 being a good mean.

Look over your hierarchy with these points in mind. You may need to add or delete scenes to meet these guidelines. And, don't despair if your first hierarchy doesn't look perfect. Just try again. The first is the hardest. A point to remember: A poor hierarchy may mean poor results. You'll find the time you spend designing a good list will be well worth it later on.

Step Five: Stack The Deck. With your finished hierarchy shining brightly before you, list each scene on a separate 3 x 5 index card. Arrange a "deck" of these cards with the least anxiety-producing scene on top and the one with the highest suds level on the bottom. This will make the scenes easy to reach during the actual desensitization procedure, allowing you to be a bit more flexible in changing, adding, or deleting items as you go through your program.

After you've finished these five steps, go back over

your hierarchy. If it looks good, you deserve a round of applause. If it doesn't, work your way back through the steps until you've solved the problems. Once you've gotten your hierarchy under your belt, and brushed up on the relaxation exercises from Chapter Five, you're ready to start desensitizing your phobia.

APPLYING SYSTEMATIC DESENSITIZATION TO YOUR PHOBIA

Now that you've made up your hierarchy, and learned the tricks of relaxing deeply, you should be ready to begin the actual desensitization part of the program. Begin by planning how often you'll apply the program. We suggest at least twice a week.

You'll find a checklist (see Appendix 2) that'll help you keep track of your progress through the program. It lists the various tasks in the technique, such as: building the hierarchy, mastering the exercises, and so on. The form also has space for you to record what goes on during each session, such as: the number of times you imagine each scene, how many suds you feel, etc. It's quite important to track your progress on this form as you go, so that you can see where you've been and where you're going.

Read the following instructions fully, making sure you understand them *before* you try your first session.

PREPARING

Arrange to be in a quiet room where no one will bother you when you prepare for each session. You may have to kick out your roommates, lover(s), kids, spouse, even your pets, for a while, but any noise will disrupt your relaxing and make it harder for you to imagine the scenes. Have either a tape-recorded or written version of the exercises near at hand. Put your deck of hierarchy cards in order with the first scene being the one with the lowest suds score. Have your checklist handy so you can record the results of your session as you finish.

Sit down in an easy chair or lounge, getting as comfortable as you can, and begin the following steps.

STEPS IN DESENSITIZATION
Step One: Relax Fully. Get completely relaxed. Take as long as you need to do this. After a while, you'll be able to relax in just a few minutes, though at first it may take longer. *Don't* go on to the next step until you're fully relaxed. Just think about relaxing deeply, and enjoy.

Step Two: Visualize the Hierarchy Scene. Once you're completely relaxed, turn to your first card—the one with the lowest suds level. Remaining as relaxed as you can, imagine the scene as clearly as possible for about ten seconds. Concentrate on relaxing completely as you imagine the scene. After ten seconds, stop visualizing.

If you felt *no anxiety* when you visualized (less than five suds), you're ready for the next scene. But before you pick up the next card, relax for about two minutes. Then, repeat step two with this next card. If you felt more than five suds of anxiety, go to step three.

Step Three: Regain Relaxation, And reimagine the Scene. (Use this step only if you felt more than five suds of anxiety.) Turn your card face-down and relax deeply. Relax for two or three minutes, or however long it takes to gain a fully relaxed state. Now, pick up the scene again and imagine it for ten seconds more. Concentrate on remaining relaxed the whole time you're doing this. Then stop the scene. If you still feel more than five suds of anxiety, repeat this step once again. If you felt no discomfort, relax for a moment and move on to the next scene, going back to Step Two.

Do this with each card in your hierarchy. Notice that you never go on to the next scene until you can visualize the one before without anxiety. And don't rush or worry if you don't feel you're going fast enough. Take your time. You may have to imagine a certain scene a number of times before you're able to relax properly. But, sooner or later you'll be able to visualize high suds scenes without feeling anxious. At this point, you'll be ready to go on to the next card.

Step Four: Keep Track Of Your Progress. At the end of your session, complete your checklist. Record the scenes you visualized, the number of times you did and the suds levels you experienced.

SOME HINTS AND GUIDELINES

The following are a few hints to use as general guidelines. Read them carefully, and make sure you understand them.

1. Relax for 20 minutes before each session. You can reduce this later to whatever length of time you need, but make sure you're totally relaxed before you begin visualizing. *This is very important.*

2. Begin each new session by thinking about the last hierarchy scene that didn't cause anxiety in the past session. If you feel discomfort, go back to the previous scenes, until you reach one where you don't feel anxious. Then, go on from there.

3. After each scene, don't think of anything but relaxing. Do this for about two minutes before going on.

4. You should imagine each scene at least twice, even if the scene doesn't cause anxiety on the first try.

5. If you find that you can't completely relax during a session, stop. Try it again later, when conditions are better.

6. Plan for your session to last 20 to 30 minutes past the time you need to become initially relaxed. Don't be upset if you can only view one or two scenes a session without getting tense. Each person has his own rate. Some move quickly at the beginning of the hierarchy and slow down at

121

the end. It may be the reverse for others. In any case, remember to take your time. Enjoy what you're doing and the results your efforts promise.

7. If you do have a scene which causes major problems, you may be trying to go too fast. You might have too large a suds difference between that scene and the one before it. If so, design a new item whose suds value falls between the two, and try that one first.

NOW THAT YOU'VE FINISHED THE HIERARCHY...

Once you're done with this part of the SD technique, you'll probably feel far more comfortable and at ease in thinking about your particular phobic object. But to make it complete, you need to begin making attempts to actually *encounter* the object, the thing that once made you white with fear.

Being able to visualize about your phobic object or situation in the comfort of your living room is one thing. Encountering the situation "in the flesh" may be another. Granted you've come a long way to get this far, especially if your phobia was an intense one. And if you can now calmly visualize a hierarchy item that used to cause 90 to 100 suds, you've done an admirable job. But it isn't over until you can look your phobic stimulus in the face, whatever it may be, and say *"You don't scare me anymore!"*

Carolyn Rhinehart, the young lady whose dog phobia was described at the start of this chapter, successfully carried out a self-directed SD program, using steps just like those above. After completing the procedure, she wondered how she'd feel when she now saw a dog. She wasn't kept in suspense for long, though. Not more than a few days later, she found herself walking past a pet store. And the front window was filled with dogs.

At first, the thought of going up to the window freaked me out a little. I guess I still didn't believe the fear was gone. But then I became curious about what'd happen if I did. So, I did it. I was a little nervous at first, but the feeling quickly vanished, leaving in its place a feeling of. . . well, feeling of freedom, I guess. Even though it wasn't any big deal, the dogs being behind the window and all, I still felt kinda proud. Yes, proud of myself for beating this thing. Cause I knew right then I'd never run in fear from a dog again. Unless, of course, he was chasing me.

So Carolyn beat her phobia, just as you can beat yours. And she went out and took steps to prove it to herself, by facing the dogs.

As you go out to expose yourself to your once-phobic stimulus or situation, we suggest doing it gradually. Approach it slowly, and in steps, similar to your hierarchy. And if you find yourself becoming anxious, back up, relax and try it again, just as you did in imagining the scenes.

We think you'll find, in doing this, that it's far easier than you think to beat your phobia; that the intense fear you once felt will slowly ebb, leaving a sea of calm in its wake, freeing you from the constraints it once put on your life.

For good.

SYSTEMATIC DESENSITIZATION CHECKLIST

Name _____ Date _____

Specific Fear Response _____

	Tasks	Date
1.	Achieved skill in deep muscle relaxation	_____
2.	Developed systematic desensitization hierarchy	_____
3.	Checked hierarchy and made suggested or needed changes.	_____
4.	Developed ability to visualize scenes	_____

5. Record of systematic desensitization. Directions: Write the date and number of the session in the far left column, the number of the scene being visualized in the second column and the number of times the scene was visualized in the third column. Record one scene per line. Indicate the level of discomfort produced during each visualization of any specific scene by writing in a number from 0 to 100 in the column on the far right. Zero means no discomfort, 100 means the highest degree of discomfort. Note: Each scene should be imagined enough times so that on its last visualization it produces *no* feeling of discomfort, or one no greater than *five* suds.

Date and Session Number	Scene Number	Number of Visualizations	Discomfort Level During Each Visualization (0 to 100 suds)

CHAPTER**EIGHT**

CONQUERING SOCIAL FEARS

The singular, most important thing that separates us from all other animals on this planet is our incredibly complex social network. We live on our relationships with others, eating, drinking and breathing social rewards. But in a time where society has reached an all-time high in development, in technology, in media and communication, more and more people seem to be plagued with social anxiety, a bothersome fear felt in social interactions that hinders our relations with others, stumping our ability to get the kinds of things we all need.

Like David Smith, the young man we looked at in the first chapter. David felt like he never knew what to say, what to do, how to react, how to talk to others and get them to talk to him. So, when faced with a social interaction, especially with new people, he became acutely uncomfortable. Fear and arousal swelled up inside, making him feel awkward, stilted and embarrassed when he tried to talk with someone.

Why is David like this?

SOCIAL PHOBIAS VERSUS SOCIAL FEAR: ANXIETY, OR NOT KNOWING WHAT TO DO?

There are two reasons why a person may have trouble interacting with others as well as he or she would like.

Social Phobias: Inhibition By Anxiety. First, the person may *know* what to say or do, but for some reason or another, is too anxious to carry it out. A good example of this is the fear of speaking in front of large groups of people, something we've probably all felt at one time or another. Here, the person knows what to say, generally has a speech prepared, but becomes so uptight that the presentation comes off poorly.

Take Joseph Atwood, for instance.

Joseph was a very successful businessman, who'd done well nearly all his life in whatever he tried to do. He had a family, got along admirably with others and was liked by his friends and associates. Socially, he was friendly, charming, assertive and outgoing. He wasn't shy, nor did he show signs of social anxiety.

Except this one: Whenever Joseph has to speak in front of a group of more than just a few people, his fear response kicked on, full power, immobilizing him with paralyzing arousal. For almost his whole career, he'd been amazingly adept at avoiding having to do any public speaking, which prevented his experiencing this fear very often. But it also kept him from trying it out and thereby learning that he *could* do it, and that there was really no basis for his apprehension.

Now, the gig was up. He was up against the wall, with no way out. He *had* to give a report before the Community Dealers Association, and he was panicked.

Social Phobias, SD and Behavioral Rehearsal. There are two ways of overcoming this kind of social phobia, where the person knows the responses, has the skills, but is inhibited by anxiety. One is systematic desensitization, the technique for phobic fear we described in the last chapter. The situation causing the fear is very specific (public speaking) and it'd be easy to draw up a hierarchy for it.

Another technique often used along with SD is *Behavioral Rehearsal*, which is what I used with Joseph. Here's how it works:

"Is there anything you can do to help me? I'll do anything you say, anything at all."

"Okay, Joseph, I think I can help you beat this thing, if you're serious about following my instructions."

"Of course, just name it."

"What I want you to do, then, is to stand up, right here, imagining you're in front of the community group, and give your speech."

"Ah, I...I don't know if I can. I'd feel foolish doing that," he replied, a slight bit indignant.

"Listen, Joseph, I'm not trying to make a fool out of you, or embarrass you in any way. But you asked me to help you, and that's how I plan to do it. You see, if you practice your speech this way, imagining you're really in front of an audience, I think you'll find that your fear will subside a bit. Just try it, all right?"

He thought for a few seconds, then shrugged his shoulders. *"Okay, what the hell. You're the boss."*

He stood up, straightened his jacket, squared of his shoulders, and began.

"I would...ah...I'd like to take...just a...ah, just a few...ah hell, doctor, I can't do it. I feel so stupid!"

"Look, Joseph, better you should screw up now, here in my office, than on Saturday in front of the community group. Now come on, quit messing around and let's go!"

He started again with his report, this time making it all the way through, despite some embarrassed pauses and other stumbles. But the important thing was he made it through.

"You know," he said, a trace of a smile beginning to appear, *"toward the end I didn't feel too uptight, Doc.*

He rehearsed the report three more times in my office, the last of which came off pretty smoothly. I told him to go over it several times with his family, and then come in again the day before the meeting. When he did, the session went well, and he'd obviously done his homework. He rehearsed it a few more times, and it actually sounded good.

The big day came, and Joseph delivered his talk, successfully, feeling only a small amount of anxiety.

Behavioral rehearsal is a good technique for getting rid of fear that's become tied up with various social responses, a nice method of practicing what you already know how to do, but are anxious about, until you find yourself able to put if off calmly, with self-assurance and confidence. We've probably all used it, at least to ourselves, imagining what we're going to say to someone, or what we're going to do in a particular situation. Have you ever come home and told your spouse how you're going to walk into your boss's office the next day and ask him or her for that raise you've been wanting? Or graphically described to a friend what you were going to tell that jerk who keeps getting on your nerves? By actually going through the response, *out loud,* you'll find that eventually you can do it with less fear or anger than if you hadn't practiced it.

Behavioral rehearsal also helps us learn *new* social skills we didn't know before, allowing us to practice until we can do them with no problem, making it a valuable tool in overcoming the second kind of social anxiety, the kind that's caused by simply *not knowing what to do.*

Social Fear: Being afraid because you don't know what to do. In social phobias the person knows what to do, but is afraid to do it. Social fear, on the other hand, involves being uptight socially because you *don't know* what to do—you don't have the social skills you need for comfortable social exchanges. This is the kind of fear that grips David Smith, along with many others among us.

While the socially phobic person has to overcome anxiety tied to a particular response, like Joseph Atwood's fear of public speaking, the socially fearful must learn *new* responses, *new* patterns of behavior that'll help them interact successfully with others. Like learning how to start and end conversations, how to make small-talk, how to say "no" when you want to, how to look calm and self-confident while talking to someone, and so on. In this chapter, we've put together instructions you can follow to learn these skills, to practice them and then to try out your new social repertoire on others.

HOW ARE YOUR SOCIAL SKILLS?

Below, you'll find a list of the various behaviors that are important in successful social interactions. Go through the list, and rate yourself on these skills. This will help you know which skills you already have, and which ones you might need to work on.

SOCIAL SKILLS CHECKLIST

This is a checklist to help you identify areas of your social behavior that you want to improve. For each skill listed, check in the appropriate place whether you feel you have the skill and use it (GOOD), you're not sure about it (NOT SURE), or whether you really don't have the skill (NEEDS WORK).

VERBAL SKILLS	*GOOD*	*NOT SURE*	*NEEDS WORK*
1. Loudness of voice			
2. Speech fluency			
3. Use of the pronoun "I"			
4. Paying compliments			
5. Expressing affection			
6. Expressing empathy			
7. Giving greetings to others			
8. Starting conversations			
9. Keeping conversations going			
10. Maintaining control of conversations			
11. Stopping conversations			
12. Small talk			
13. Talking about yourself			
14. Expressing your feelings			
15. Expressing your emotions			
16. Agreeing with compliments			
17. Disagreeing with others			
18. Asking "why?"			
19. Making requests			
20. Saying "No"			

NONVERBAL SKILLS	*GOOD*	*NOT SURE*	*NEEDS WORK*
21. Eye contact with others			
22. Posture			
23. Distance from others when interacting			
24. Facial expressions			
25. Hand and other body movements			

Now, make a note of all the skills you checked "not sure" or "needs work." These are the ones you should pay particular attention to as we go through the various social behaviors—what they are, why they're useful, and how to learn them.

To further examine where you stand in terms of social skills, we've included another form for you to complete, the Rathus Assertiveness schedule. This scale was developed by S. A. Rathus in 1973,[12] and has been used all over the country in studies of assertiveness. To fill it out, just assign a value to each statement by choosing a value number from the code at the top of the scale, picking the number that describes you best. Write these numbers in the blanks by each statement.

To figure out your score, add up the values you've given the statements, *reversing* the sign of the value numbers for statements *followed by an asterisk* (*). For all the other statements the sign stays the same.

To evaluate your score, compare it with these norms:

RATHUS ASSERTIVENESS SCHEDULE

Directions: Indicate how characteristic or descriptive each of the following statements is of you by using the code given below.

> +3 very characteristic of me, extremely descriptive
> +2 rather characteristic of me, quite descriptive
> +1 somewhat characteristic of me, slightly descriptive
> -1 somewhat uncharacteristic of me, slightly nondescriptive
> -2 rather uncharacteristic of me, quite nondescriptive
> -3 very uncharacteristic of me, extremely nondescriptive

___ 1. Most people seem to be more aggressive and assertive than I am.*

___ 2. I have hesitated to make or accept dates because of "shyness."

___ 3. When the food served at a restaurant is not done to my satisfaction, I complain about it to the waiter or waitress.

___ 4. I am careful to avoid hurting other people's feelings, even when I feel that I have been injured.*

___ 5. If a salesman has gone to considerable trouble to show me merchandise which is not quite suitable, I have a difficult time in saying "No."*

___ 6. When I am asked to do something, I insist upon knowing why.

___ 7. There are times when I look for a good, vigorous argument.

___ 8. I strive to get ahead as well as most people in my position.

___ 9. To be honest, people often take advantage of me.*

___10. I enjoy starting conversations with new acquaintances and strangers.

___11. I often don't know what to say to attractive persons of the opposite sex.*

___12. I will hesitate to make phone calls to business establishments and institutions.*

___13. I would rather apply for a job or for admission to a college by writing letters than by going through with personal interviews.*

___14. I find it embarrassing to return merchandise.*

___15. If a close and respected relative were annoying me, I would smother my feelings rather than express my annoyance.*

___16. I have avoided asking questions for fear of sounding stupid.*

___17. During an argument I am sometimes afraid that I will get so upset that I will shake all over.*

___18. If a famed and respected lecturer makes a statement which I think is incorrect, I will have the audience hear my point of view as well.

___19. I avoid arguing over prices with clerks and salesmen.*

___20. When I have done something important or worthwhile, I manage to let others know about it.

___21. I am open and frank about my feelings.

___22. If someone has been spreading false and bad stories about me, I see him (her) as soon as possible to "have a talk" about it.

___23. I often have a hard time saying "No."*

___24. I tend to bottle up my emotions rather than make a scene.*

___25. I complain about poor service in a restaurant and elsewhere.

___26. When I am given a compliment, I sometimes just don't know what to say.*

___27. If a couple near me in a theatre or at a lecture were conversing rather loudly, I would ask them to be quiet or to take their conversation elsewhere.

___28. Anyone attempting to push ahead of me in a line is in for a good battle.

___29. I am quick to express an opinion.

___30. There are times when I just can't say anything.*

These norms are based on studies done with college students, so if you're not one, the norm won't be exact. But in general, if your score is 20 or more points *below* the norm for your sex, you should pay close attention to the assertive behaviors we'll discuss in this chapter, especially responses like *saying "no," making requests, expressing your feelings, expressing your emotions, disagreeing with others,* and so on.

OVERCOMING ANXIETY THROUGH BECOMING SOCIALLY SKILLED[13]

Now that you have some idea what areas you'll be needing to work on, let's get started. For each type of skill, we'll explain what it is, give examples if appropriate, tell you why it's useful and important in social exchanges and give you suggestions as to how to go about learning it. But, read the whole chapter before trying to learn the skills, so you'll have a good overview of the whole repertoire we're covering.

We're going to start out by looking at "conversational" skills, responses that will help you more comfortably start, maintain and end conversations with others. We'll cover a variety of different kinds of these, including how to say "no" when you want to, and what to say when making requests of others. Throughout this section, you'll notice that we emphasize, and encourage, taking on an assertive, self-confident manner, an active, direct role in social exchange, one that'll help you stand up for yourself and for your rights as a person, instead of becoming anxious, buckling under and giving in when confronted by others. Keep this confident, self-assured stance firmly in mind as you work your way through the rest of this chapter.

The skills we discuss aren't hard to learn, but they will require effort and practice on your part to really master. And in the beginning, you may find that practicing them makes you somewhat anxious. If this happens, just back off and relax awhile. By now, you probably have the deep muscle relaxation techniques (Chapter Five) down pat, so make use of them to fight any arousal that comes up. Also, if you get hung up on any particular skill and feel too uptight to try it, use the systematic desensitization technique (Chapter Seven) to weaken this fear to the point where you *can* practice the skill. In many cases, social fear seems to involve a phobic component combined with not knowing what to do. So, often a combined SD - social skills approach is a good idea.

Above all, be sure to practice these responses as often as you can. We saw how the behavioral rehearsal technique helped Joseph Atwood pull off his speech successfully. The same thing can work for you, if you let it. Simply knowing rationally, consciously, isn't enough—you've got to actually make the responses and use them as much as you can in your everyday life, until they become second nature to you. Even in the face of fear, keep trying the skills. Because only by doing this can you begin to chip away the dread, the apprehension, the uncomfortable social anxiety that's been standing, not so silently, in the wings for so long.

Conversational Skills

A very important part of the social skills story revolves around the ability to "shoot the breeze." Making friends, meeting new people, interesting and stimulating interactions with others all depend on your ability to talk easily and comfortably. Unfortunately, to the many people who're socially fearful, this may be one of the hardest things in the world to do, making most social encounters difficult, awkward, embarrassing and anxiety-producing. Like our David Smith at the office party (Chapter One), their responses in conversations often consist of one-word answers and agreeing with what's being said, instead of contributing to the discussion, expressing their opinions and generally investing themselves in the exchange. Or, instead of being quiet and reserved, some socially fearful folk overcompensate, becoming loud, boisterous, aggressive and obnoxious, which tends to offend others.

Social Skill #1: Starting Conversations. One of the tallest hurdles we have to clear in the fight against social inhibition is learning how to approach another person and start a conversation. It isn't easy, especially for the socially anxious, and learning how to do this is a gradual process. But if you hang in, you *can* learn it and open many new doors for your social life.

Start by listing various ways of striking up conversations, "openers" you can use to get another person talking. Looking through a newspaper can give you a bunch of interesting tidbits you can use to initiate conversations, like: "Hey, Ed, did you read in the paper about the guy who won 64,000 bucks with a sweepstakes ticket he found in the subway?"; or "Say, have you seen *The Omen II* yet? I read a review in the Herald saying it was pretty good."

Once you've collected several openers, go ahead and try them out. Start with practicing on your friends and relatives until you feel comfortable enough to try striking up a conversation with someone you don't know as well. As you first begin to try this out, don't be too concerned about the topic of conversation—just try to approach someone else and say something. Reward yourself for every conversation you start, even if it doesn't go beyond that point.

Also, keep these thoughts in mind. First, you're not the only person in the world who's a little anxious about starting conversations. Lots of other folks are, too. In fact, silence among a group of people often makes everyone anxious, and once you initiate talking, breaking the ice, they all feel more comfortable. Second, not everybody you run into may want to talk. If your opener falls on its face, don't consider this a defeat or insult. At this point, look at it as a success, because after all, you *attempted to get a conversation going,* which is what you're working on at this point. If it doesn't pan out, well that's the way it goes sometimes. Third, you'll probably be a little uptight as you attempt to initiate conversations with people you don't know very well. This isn't at all unusual. It will pass the more often you try it and the better you get. If you find yourself getting overly wired, just sit back for a moment and run through a short relaxation exercise. Take a few deep breaths and concentrate on something peaceful and relaxing before trying again. A few minutes of relaxation can do wonders in cutting down this arousal. And fourth, it's a good idea to keep a record of how you're coming along with your practice. This way, you're able to closely watch your progress, and you'll probably find yourself practicing more often. A chart like the following example works fine for this:

Social Skills Progress Chart

Date	Skill	Anxiety Felt					
		None	1	2	3	4	5 Extreme
	Initiating Conversations						
6/14	"	1	2	(3)	4		5
	"	1	2	3	(4)		5
	"	1	(2)	3	4		5
	"	1	(2)	3	4		5
6/15	"	1	2	(3)	4		5
	"	1	2	(3)	4		5
	"	1	(2)	3	4		5
	"	1	(2)	3	4		5
	"	1	2	(3)	4		5
		1	2	3	4		5
		1	2	3	4		5
		1	2	3	4		5
		1	2	3	4		5

In this sample, we see that on 6/14, our person practiced starting conversations four times, feeling anxiety ranging from 2 to 4 in intensity. On 6/15, five attempts were made, with anxiety ranging from 2 to 3. **Social Skill #2: Maintaining A Conversation.** Now that you've begun to overcome your fear of starting a conversation, and made attempts at initiating talking, how do you keep the discussion from dying once you've got it off the ground? How do you avoid the awkward and embarrassing lulls we've all come to know and dread so much, *after* the ice is broken?

One way to stimulate another person's talking is by *actively listening,* showing that you're interested in what's being said. This seems like an obvious point, but many people will ask a question or otherwise begin a conversation, and just stand there, shuffling their feet, looking around the room, never commenting on what's being said, thereby effectively killing the conversation as clearly and quickly as if they'd shot it with an elephant gun.

One way to show a person you care about what they're saying is to use *minimal encouragers.* These brief, simple phrases do just what their name implies— they encourage the person to keep on talking. A few examples: "That's so true." "That's a very interesting point." "Yes, I've felt that way myself." "That's incredible."

Minimal encouragers also include things like using facial expression, nodding your head, smiling at the speaker, maintaining eye-contact, and using comments like "oh," "uh-huh," "hmmm," and so on— small, sometimes subtle ways of showing the speaker that you're listening to what he or she is saying, and that it's interesting to you. They can make a dramatic difference in how the speaker responds (or doesn't respond) to you.

Here's a little exercise you can do for yourself to

What do you think of nuclear power plants as a means of overcoming the energy crisis?

illustrate the power of minimal encouragers. Get a friend, or your spouse, to sit down with you for a couple of minutes. Ask them to simply remain expressionless, looking at the floor, while you talk for a minute or two about what you've done that day. Now, repeat what you said, only this time, have your partner respond using frequent minimal encouragers. Notice a difference in how you felt during the two episodes? Were you a little more uncomfortable during the first, perhaps feeling like you were talking to a *brick wall?* Well, unless you use minimal encouragers, chances are that's how people who talk to *you* feel.

Compile a list of all the minimal encouragers you can think of, adding to those we've listed above. If you have trouble coming up with them, watch other people, and note the ones they use. Or watch some talk shows on the tube—TV hosts typically use a variety of minimal encouragers to stimulate talking by the guests.

Once you have a list, practice them every time you find yourself in a conversation, using as many as you comfortably can. If you haven't used them before, or used very few, you'll probably notice an immediate change in how people relate to you in conversation. They'll be more talkative, friendlier and will not doubt act like they're enjoying themselves. Keep practicing until you're able to use them without thinking about it, making encouragers an automatic part of your conversational repertoire. You'll be glad you did, and so will your friends.

In trying to keep a conversation going, it's a good idea to ask questions that stimulate your listener to talk. *Closed-ended* questions are those that have very specific answers, and can usually be responded to with just one or two words, like "Yes" or "No." For example: "Are you going to the office party this weekend?" (Yes or No) "Did you like that Bogart movie on the tube last night?" (Yes or No) Although people sometimes go on to elaborate on their answers, closed-ended questions don't necessarily prompt them to do so.

On the other hand, *open-ended* questions specifically ask for an opinion, a description, a feeling or information, encouraging answers that are quite a bit lengthier and more elaborate than closed-ended questions. Like: "What've you been doing since I saw you last?" or "Hey, Joni, you've been to Europe. *Tell me a little* about what it's like in Paris."

As you can see, there's really no way to answer an open-ended question with just one or two words. They're great for breaking the ice, and for getting people to talk about their opinions, their feelings and themselves.

Talk-show hosts, like Johnny Carson, Merv Griffin, Dinah Shore, David Frost and Dick Cavett, are *masters* at welding open-ended questions. In watching their shows, you'll see these questions being used quite frequently, prompting guest responses that're interesting to the audience, revealing, candid, and that show their style of humor, interests and personalities. They also tend to keep the guests talking, and the show rolling.

Your listeners' answers to open-ended questions can be a rich source of information about their interests, what they like to do, the kinds of things they enjoy and the sort of person they are. If you're a good listener, you'll be able to glean quite a lot from this, like interests you've got in common with them, ideas and opinions you might want to add to yourself, as well as things you may want to know more about, all of which you can use to help keep the conversation going.

Make a list of open-ended questions and try them out in your daily conversations. Although you may find it hard to think them up at first, particularly in discussions, the more you use them, the more easily they'll come to you.

Don't rely completely, however, on minimal encouragers and open-ended questions to keep the ball rolling. If you do, your partner's going to feel like he or she's being interrogated. Whenever you hear something that stimulates an idea or two, add them to the discussion. Although many people like to hear themselves talk, this gets old. So step in with your own comments whenever you can. We'll talk further about expressing your own opinions a little later on in this chapter.

Social Skill #3: Maintaining Control Of A Conversation. Closely related to a fear of starting a conversation and keeping it going, is the fear of maintaining control of the conversation. Many folks feel that whenever they've got something to add to a discussion, they've got to add it immediately, usually interrupting the speaker. For most people, being interrupted isn't much of a problem, but someone who's socially anxious to begin with may view this as a slap in the face, a statement that what they were saying wasn't worth hearing. In these cases being interrupted increases fear activation, making the speaker surrender the role of talking without a whimper, feeling perhaps that he or she's not entitled to speak out if anyone else tries to take the floor.

The fact is, you are entitled to say whatever you want. If you're interrupted, stand up and regain your place in the conversation. You can do this by just continuing to talk despite the interruption, speaking *louder* than you were, until the interrupter realizes his or her infringement on your point, or by waiting until the interrupter finishes talking, and then returning to what you were saying, ignoring the interrupting comments.

But the best way to handle this situation is to simply ask if the person would mind if you finished your point, adding that you'd be glad to listen to what they had to say *after* you've finished.

Social Skill #4: Making Small Talk. Perhaps the greatest difficulty many socially anxious people face is in making small talk—speaking that's composed and uttered on the spur of the moment, the volunteering of comments, expressions of feelings, giving information, relating an experience or just describing a situation. Small talk requires the spontaneity and freedom that anxiety often denies a person, the ability to state thoughts without being asked, without hesitation, timidity, or fear of being ridiculed. It's simply talking freely about whatever comes into your head.

But social anxiety tends to make people *listeners* rather than talkers, passive rather than active participants in many conversations. How do you overcome this?

By learning to talk more! It's as simple as that. Talk to a friend, your spouse, even yourself. The important thing is that you get experience in talking for longer and longer periods of time. Start by talking for short periods—ten, twenty seconds to begin with—about anything that comes into your mind, anything at all. Just be sure to talk for the whole period. Once you can comfortably do this, gradually increase these periods by fifteen or twenty seconds until you can make small talk for seven to ten minutes with your partner. If you start feeling anxious, stop and relax. Run through the exercises from Chapter Five before trying again. But keep practicing until you can talk for ten minutes without getting anxious or uncomfortable.

Once you can do *this,* you're ready to go ahead and start trying small talk as the opportunity comes up in your day-to-day experiences.

Just remember, the key to making small talk is to *stay relaxed,* just be yourself, and let the talk flow from that. When you reach the point where you can easily achieve this, talking off your cuff won't be a problem for you.

Social Skill #5: Expressing Your Emotions. Have you ever caught yourself listening to a lot of inane banter, ridiculous stuff, but nonetheless nodding your head like a wooden puppet in agreement just to keep the conversation rolling? Or going through all kinds of changes to encourage a person to lay a bunch of gibberish on you that you really don't want to hear anyway?

Emotional dishonesty characterizes this type of interaction—exchanges made by folks who are a little afraid to disagree with whoever's talking, a bit anxious about expressing their emotions with regard to a particular motion or topic of conversation. It's not hard to get caught up in this, playing a perpetual guessing game, forever trying to read the expressions of others and slant your behavior accordingly, rarely stating your true feelings, going out of your way, even against the grain, to please the speaker. Now, this style may make whoever's talking feel good and maybe cause them to think that you're a great listener. But the end results is a lack of real communication between the people involved in the conversation.

For meaningful social interactions, there has to be an element of *emotional honesty*. If you deny your own feelings in an exchange, molding your reactions like play-dough into whatever shape you think might be effective in rewarding the speaker, you'll find yourself falling into a rut that can be pretty hard to get out of.

Let's talk about negative feelings and emotions for a minute. It's not at all unusual for the shy, socially timid person to hide anger, resentment and hostility generated by an interaction, because they feel it's "out of place" to express such feelings. And after several years of denial they may find it rather easy to do this, but not without a price: a foul, smoldering frustration that may find vent in an outburst of inappropriate aggression, or less directly, in an increase in blood pressure, heart trouble, or an ulcer. We've all read in the papers about some "nice quiet boy" suddenly going off the "deep end" and randomly shooting the hell out of people. But more commonly, we find those who silently smolder, burning, simmering, waiting for a change, an opportunity to blow up in a fit of temper, blasting out all the suppressed emotion they failed to put in their interactions, the anger they hated themselves for keeping inside.

The point is, being honest with others and, more importantly, with ourselves, plays a major role in letting out these emotions as they arise, rather than after they've been stored up, festering like poorly jarred tomatoes for months or even years. It can make us feel far more comfortable with ourselves, knowing that we're expressing what we feel, as we're feeling it.

We're not saying that you should get up and fly into a rage whenever someone says something that you don't agree with, or fall all over yourself in lavish praise over something that you do. We're simply stating that one part of a good conversation is emotional honesty on the part of the participants. And accurately expressing your emotions is an adaptive, useful skill, however you want to cut the cake. It'll not only make others respond to you more positively and directly, but it'll do wonders for your own feelings about yourself, your integrity, your *likability*.

So, instead of being emotionally bland and noncommittal, take a shot at expressing your feelings, adding emotional spice to your expressions, a little "feeling talk."

Social Skill #6: Showing Your Feelings. "Feeling talk" is a term originated by the notable psychologist Andrew Salter,[14] who is considered by many as one of the leading founders of contemporary behavior therapy. It involves being able to honestly express our feelings—a tremendously rewarding skill. It makes us feel good, and can add a touch of flavor to otherwise bland expressions. One of our goals in developing better social skills is to overcome the anxiety that's associated with "feeling-talk" for many people. The best way to do this is to practice it—start including your feelings in your conversations whenever you can. Practice doing this until you no longer feel uptight or self-conscious about using feeling talk. Here's some examples of different feeling-statements, along with their corresponding feeling states, put together by Mr. Salter:

Feeling Talk Remarks	Type of Feeling Talk
1. I like the snow scene. It makes me feel cool to look at it.	Like
2. I detest that man and everything he stands for.	Dislike
3. That shade of green is perfect for you.	Praise
4. You're looking fine!	Praise.
5. This is Friday. I thought it would never get here.	Relief.
6. You can't do this to me!	Complaint
7. I'll wait, even if it kills me.	Determination
8. My feet hurt.	Discomfort
9. The desk set was just what I needed.	Appreciation
10. I wonder what happens in the next installment.	Curiosity
11. You don't expect me to believe that, do you?	Skepticism
12. I'm not afraid of him. I don't care if he does his damndest.	Courage
13. I'm going to keep punching until I win.	Determination
14. This meal feels fine.	Contentment
15. Good grief, I feel terrible about this.	Anguish
16. What kind of a place do you call this?	Annoyance
17. Now, that was stupid to me!	Self-criticism

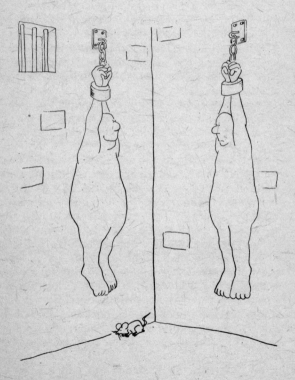

I know exactly how you feel!

Social Skill #6A: Handing Out Compliments.
Compliments, praise, approval, this is the food we all
live on, the petrol that keeps our engines running, the
thing we probably spend the most time striving for in
our culture. And giving out praise and compliments is
an extremely useful social skill. It makes other people
feel good, and can make you feel good in return. When
you see something you like, don't hide it. Express it,
with sincerity, and watch the effects it has on the
recipient.

Expressing compliments openly is a direct extension
of the emotional honesty skill we talked about above. A
well-paid compliment makes the person getting it feel
kind of nice and also has a positive effect on you, in that
you're expressing what you feel, what you think. The
more you can do *this,* the more socially at ease you'll
become.

In these days of hustling and competition, sincere
compliments are far too rare, suppressed far too often
because of petty jealousies and implicit rivalry. The
person who gives them honestly will find that others
respond most favorably to a direct statement of praise.

Social Skill #6B: Expressing Affection. This is
another response that seems to be nearing the
"endangered species" list in our increasingly
impersonal culture. Many people seem to be a shade
reluctant to "risk" expressing affection, due to their
fear of rejection by the other person involved. You're
only vulnerable, they might say, when you *expose too
much* of yourself. If you openly and honestly express
feelings of love and affection, you're giving the person
a chance to reject them, thereby rejecting *you* in the
process. So the person fearing rejection plays "hard,"
like a rock, an island. And, as Simon and Garfunkel
once put it, "a rock feels no pain/and an island never
cries."

But rocks don't have much *fun* either. I, for one,
would rather take my chances as a vulnerable person

than be "safe" as an invulnerable rock. And even the "rock" posture isn't *really* foolproof. If you fear rejection so much you can't risk trying to maintain a close relationship with another human, you're far from being free. In reality, these rocks have sot, pink underbellies, easily penetrated by the sharp edges of fear, the same fear that forms the cell they live in, ever looking, scanning, scrambling to avoid being hurt, all the while setting themselves for disaster if they ever are.

At any rate, affection isn't a form of barter, to be given with the expectation of getting something in return. It's a feeling, something you'd have even if the person did decide to reject it. In other words, affection can be expressed freely and honestly, with no strings attached, which is probably the way it should be.

How about you? Do you express affection as openly as you'd like, or are you a rock? If expressing affection makes you anxious, practice it, concentrating on staying relaxed, until you can make affectionate statements without becoming fearful.

Social Skill #6C: Expressing Empathy. Empathy is the ability to share someone else's feelings, to "sing" along with their emotional tones. Often, socially anxious people experience empathy with another, but are fearful of expressing it. Part of being socially skilled lies in being able to express these kinds of thoughts and feelings. If, after listening to a friend relate an upsetting experience you start to really know how he or she feels, share your thoughts. Your friend will appreciate it, and it will expand your repertoire of emotional expression.

Social Skill #6D: Greeting Others. How are you at greeting people? Are you someone who hardly ever gives a greeting, and who quietly and unenthusiastically responds with a grunt to greetings from others. If so, practice such greetings as "Hi!" "What's happening?" "Nice to see you!" until you can say them with *feeling*.

How does a cheerful and genuinely interested greeting from someone affect you? Does it make you feel good? Then try showing that in your response to other's greetings, as well as in your greetings to them. It's a basic, simple, easy-to-learn skill that's really useful socially.

Social Skill #7: Talking About Yourself. Out of shyness, timidity, or thinking that others would find the topic boring, many socially anxious people rarely ever talk about themselves. They often simply don't view themselves as "important" or interesting enough. Once they develop the habit of talking about themself, however, they find that their feelings of excessive modesty and shyness are replaced with self-confidence and a new sense of outgoingness.

To learn this skill, start by making yourself discuss some aspect of your life with a partner for a brief period of time, at least once a day. During this practice period, briefly take over the conversation, and talk about yourself, relating something that happened to you that day. Initially, what you say isn't all that important, as long as it's about *you*. As you grow more relaxed in doing this, gradually lengthen the amount of time you practice, until you can complete an entire period without getting anxious. At this point, begin to interject this kind of talking into your everyday conversations, and watch the change in your self-confidence.

Social Skill #8: Using The Personal Pronoun "I." This skill is closely related to Skill #7. For the same reasons shy people don't talk about themselves, they tend to find it tension-producing to use the pronoun "I" in conversation. If this applies to you, practice this skill by making it a point to identify your beliefs, feelings and desires by saying "I believe," "I feel," "I wish," and so on. As your other skills develop, this will follow suit.

Social Skill #9: Accepting Compliments. We've already discussed giving compliments (Social Skill #6A) as a form of expressing your feelings. *Accepting* compliments is also a response many socially fearful people lack.

I've seen people spend hundreds of bucks buying a fantastic outfit of clothes and jewelry, spend hours getting ready to go out, and then respond to a well-deserved compliment with: "Oh, you must be kidding! This rag? Why I'm almost embarrassed to be wearing it. . ." Responding to compliments by disagreeing with them is almost a reflex with most of us, and we shrug-off many that we really do deserve.

If you react this way to sincere compliments, try *agreeing* for a change, accepting them gracefully and with appreciation. The next time you get a compliment that sounds sincere, say "Well, yes, thank you. I just bought this coat, and I'm rather fond of its myself," or "Thank you, how nice of you to say so!" At first you might feel a little awkward, maybe even foolish or a trifle self-indulgent, but you'll soon find accepting compliments to be a fairly natural response.

Social Skill #10: Disagreeing With Others. As we've pointed out several times, socially anxious people are usually listeners rather than speakers and tend to nearly always agree with people rather than face an open difference of opinion, no matter what their own views might be. In our discussion on emotional honesty (Social Skill #6) we saw how this can lead to negative consequences, like frustration, anger and self-criticism. It's important, both in terms of emotional honesty and open, real communication, to know *how* to skillfully disagree with another person who's expressing views contrary to your own.

One way is to disagree *passively,* by simply not making a statement of agreement with what's being said. You can say nothing, or maybe even change the topic of conversation. This is easy to learn and shouldn't cause much anxiety, even initially.

Once you feel comfortable disagreeing passively, try coming right out and *actively* stating that you don't agree with what's being said. This can be done tactfully, by waiting for a lull in the conversation, and then saying something like this: "You know, I really don't agree with your view on .... I look at it this way. . . " followed by your point of view.

Start off gradually, beginning with minor issues that are pretty much neutral, and work your way up to the heavier, hotter topics. Let your own feelings set the pace—if you feel the old fear rising up, slow down and relax before carrying on.

There's one important thing to remember about active disagreement—It should be done *assertively*, with confidence and self-assurance, but not *aggressively*, to be useful. This means that you make your point without insults, hostile remarks, or personal attacks on the holder of the contrary view. Of course, there are some people with whom this isn't possible, folks so rigid and inflexible in their thinking that any challenge is seen as an attack that usually causes them to fly off the handle. Like the shy timid person, these aggressive people, would probably benefit from learning a more viable, less angry way of handling disagreement.

As in all the other social skills, practice is important here, so be sure to get plenty of it. Use the Social Skills Progress Chart to record your disagreements, and how much anxiety you felt while doing it.

Social Skill #11: Asking "Why?" After getting a $25.00 estimate for fixing the brakes on your car, you take it in to have the work done. When you pick it up, the mechanic hands you a bill for $52.95. *What would you do?* You get a water bill from the utility company in the mail, saying you owe $18.00 for this month's water. Your usual bill is $8.00, and you haven't used any more water this month than usual. *What would you do?*

Many socially anxious people would just pay the mechanic, and the water company, rather than trying to find out *why* the bills were so high. They seem to feel it's offensive or rude to do this, or they simply don't know *what to say* in these situations.

In cases where you want to get an explanation for something rather than letting it slide, just *ask* for it.

Why? A simple question, but all that can save you a lot of trauma, self-depreciation, guilt, not to mention money, if you make use of it.

You can work on this skill by first writing down several situations where you wanted to ask "why," but didn't. Once you've listed them, write down what you'd like to say. Make your questions clear, concise, and friendly, but *firm*; and try to avoid using hostile comments in your response.

Now pratice them with a partner taking the role of the other person, rehearsing them until you can respond without feeling anxious or embarassed.

Social Skill #12: Saying "no." You've invited some people over and while you're madly dashing around the house trying to straighten things up a bit, you hear the doorbell ring. You're greeted by an aggressive young man who tells you he'd like a few minutes to introduce you to a brand-new line of encyclopedias. *What would you do?*

You're walking briskly through an airport, headed for your flight, when a young man with a shaved head approaches you, wearing a curious smile and dressed in clothing bearing an amazing likeness to old sheets. He pins a flower to your lapel, and grins at you, joyously asking for a dollar donation to help him continue spreading cheer and good faith throughout the world. *What would you do?*

Can you say "no" to unreasonable requests, or do you give in to almost anything? Do you let pesky salespeople, solicitors, friends and relatives take advantage of your good nature, or are you able to put your foot down, drawing the line at things you don't really want to do?

Saying "no" to unreasonable requests is a skill many people don't have. As a result, they get run over, chewed up and spit out by society, ending up plagued by anxiety, feelings of social inadequacy and self-depreciation. We all have the right to refuse requests that demand things we don't want to give, within reason, of course. But exercising that right is another matter—it takes effort, especially if you're someone who rarely says "no." Like asking "why," having to refuse a request makes people nervous, perhaps because they think that they'll hurt somebody's feelings, or make the other person not like them (see Chapter Six, Irrational Belief #1 for a discussion of this). Others may simply not know *how* to tactfully refuse, so they become anxious and usually wind up giving in.

Actually, refusing unreasonable requests is a remarkably easy response, often consisting of a single word, *"no."* The big hurdle is the apprehension associated with the act. As in the other behaviors we've looked at, the fear surrounding standing up for yourself can be broken through by practicing saying "no" to various situations.

Write down situations that've come up in your life, unreasonable requests that you found yourself unable to refuse, even though you wanted to.

Next, write out and rehearse refusals for these situations. In your responses make sure the refusal is clear and straightforward, and try to keep yourself from getting off on irrelevant points, like "over-explaining" why you're saying "no," making compromises and hostile remarks. In other words, practice *flat refusals.*

For instance, to the encyclopedia salesman you might say, *"No, I'm not interested in buying encyclopedias,* thank you." Or, if you *are* interested, but are too busy to look at them: "I'd like to see your package, but I *don't have time now*. Can you come back tomorrow evening, instead?"

To the free spirit in the airport: *"No, I'm not going to donate a dollar* to your cause. But thanks for the flower."

Refusals can be clear and to the point without being rude, hostile, or aggressive. All it takes is practice. The more you use this skill when faced with an unreasonable request, the more comfortable you'll feel with your responses, and the better you'll feel about yourself. You may also find that others show you a bit more respect, now that *you're* exercising your right to refuse.

Social Skill #13: Making Requests. Closely akin to to saying "no" is the act of making a request, another behavior many people have trouble with. Maybe because they feel like making reasonable requests would be putting someone out, many folks go through life hardly asking for *anything*.

Now there's nothing inherently wrong with independence and self-reliance, but there are times when failing to make requests can be very much to our disadvantage. Like when the electricity company makes a hundred dollar mistake in your bill (in their favor, naturally). Is it *too much* to ask them to refigure the bill?

Obviously, to let it ride would be extremely self-defeating. Yet many people get so anxious when faced with something like this, they either avoid making the request, or they ask so apologetically that it may not even be taken seriously.

The fact of the matter is, it's *perfectly all right* for you to make reasonable requests, particularly when this involves standing up for your rights.

Some kinds of requests are better than others in actually getting the person to do what you want. The best way to ask is directly, clearly and without adding apologies, irrelevant issues, or hostile comments. Let's look at an example:

After saving up for a couple of weeks, Dan Freeman decided to go to a relatively expensive steak house to eat. He ordered a large cut, medium rare. Even his eyes were drooling as he stared tracelike at the waitress carrying the steak toward his table.

But his excitement didn't last for long. He cut into the beef, seeing that it was done all the way through, instead of medium rare like he'd ordered.

* * *

Now, consider these responses:

Example A: *"Uh, waitress, I asked for a medium rare steak. This one's done all the way through."*

Example B: *"Boy, what kinda place is this anyway? Don't they know how to cook steaks in there?"*

Example C: *"Would it be too much trouble to ask you if you might be able to get me another steak, cooked medium rare?"*

Example D: *"Waitress, I asked for my steak to be cooked medium rare—this one's well done. Please take it back and bring me another, cooked medium rare."*

Which response do you think would be the most effective in getting the waitress' cooperation? Which one would you probably use?

Example A isn't really a request, but rather a statement of the problem. These "softened" requests sometimes work, but tend to be much more effective when combined with a clear, straightforward call for action.

Example B is a typical reaction, but one that's really beside the point. Because the aim here, what Dan *wants,* is another steak. Comments like these are essentially irrelevant to this issue and probably aren't going to get him one.

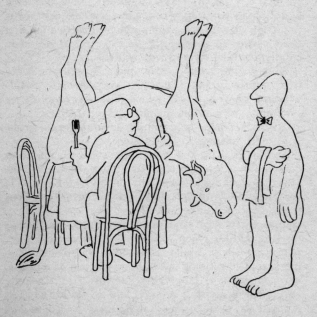

Pardon me, Waiter, but this steak seems a bit rare!

Example C is closer to a request, but the actual action called for is deeply buried in an almost apologetic style. This might work in some situations, but no doubt won't in many others, because you leave the person too much opportunity to refuse by simply saying, "Well, yes. It *would* be too much trouble."

Example D represents a straightforward, direct request, as well as a rationale, and is the sample most likely to be effective in Dan's getting another steak. It states the problem clearly, and calls for action with no apologetic tone, which is really what a good request should do.

Are there times when you have a hard time or get anxious when faced with having to make a request? If so, make a list of those situations. Now, for each situation on your list, write out a clear, nonapologetic request that will cover the problem. Practice making these requests, rehearsing until you can do them calmly, confidently and with self-assurance.

When you're ready to start making requests, begin with relatively small ones, making them to people who'll be likely to do what you ask. Then gradually try making larger ones. Remember to keep them clear and straightforward, and uncluttered by apologies, irrelevant "fillers," or aggression.

And don't worry if your requests are sometimes denied. While it's your right to make a request, it's the other person's right to deny it. Push it as far as you're comfortable going, but don't get discouraged if your requests occasionally fail.

Social Skill #14: Ending Conversations. I once worked with a client who had, for the most part, charming social skills. She asked interesting and intelligent questions, made fantastic use of minimal encouragers and other social rewards, and usually succeeded in making whoever she was talking to feel stimulated, pleasant, and well, *sociable*. There was only one thing that made her uncomfortable socially—

ending conversations. Once a conversation had started to wear a little thin, and it became obvious that it had pretty much run its course, she'd start getting nervous and usually ended up halting the discussion abruptly and awkwardly. Afterwards, she felt bad, because she'd come off to the other person as being rude. The problem was, she simply didn't know how to end a discussion gracefully.

This is a difficulty shared by many socially anxious people. They're afraid of losing the approval of the person they're talking to, so they hang around until making a closing statement really is awkward, or they abruptly terminate the conversation, running from the arousal beginning to well up in their chests. Either way, they leave cursing at themselves for not ending the discussion sooner, frustrated at not knowing how to change things.

Actually, ending conversations isn't hard. It helps to think of a variety of closing statements and practice them. A good closing statement will convey, tactfully and smoothly, that you've enjoyed the discussion, but that you really must go, giving the person the impression that you'd like to talk with them again, Examples:

Situation	Closing Statement
You've been visiting at Don's house, and feel that you've stayed long enough. You're ready to leave.	Well, Don, I've really enjoyed our conversation, but I've really got to go. I'm looking forward to seeing you again soon.
You're talking with a friend at work, but have to leave for a doctor's appointment.	I enjoyed talking to you, and would love to continue, but I've got to leave now for an appointment. See you later.
You've listened to a sales pitch for a home fire alarm unit.	Thank you for your time and effort, but I'm definitely not interested in buying a fire alarm.

If you have trouble in this area, write down several typical situations that make you anxious, and think up closing statements for them. Then practice using this technique in terminating your daily conversations.

The next skills we'll discuss have to do not so much with *what* you say as *how* you say it. Social skill involves not only doing things that'll lead to rewarding social interactions, but also doing them in a way that makes you come off as confident and self-assured, rather than shy or anxious.

Social Skill #15: Loudness Of Your Voice. The loudness with which you speak is an example of this kind of skill. How loudly we talk influences how others see us, as well as how we see ourselves. In most cases, if you speak with a faint, soft voice, you're likely to be seen as timid, or socially uncomfortable. On the other hand, bellowing loudly is also seen as a sign of discomfort on the part of a speaker. But talking with a solid, steady, easily heard tone can add to an air of being at ease, and of confidence in what you're saying.

There are exceptions to this, however. Some people "speak softly and carry a big stick," meaning that even though their voice is low, they're still listened to. And in many situations, such as intimate conversation, a soft voice might be very much to your advantage. But for the most part, speaking quietly is typically seen as indicative of shyness and a lack of confidence in what you're saying.

How loud do you need to speak? You can usually tell by watching the people you talk to. Are they "tuning you out," not really paying attention to you, or asking you to repeat things rather often? Or, are they standing back, possibly flinching, because of your excessively loud speech? How loud do you speak?

Generally you should talk loud enough to be easily heard in conversations, even if there's a lot of surrounding noise. Others shouldn't have to ask you to repeat something because they didn't hear it.

You can modify your speech volume by talking into a mirror from about ten feet away. Imagine there's someone standing at the mirror, and then speak so that person could comfortably hear what you're saying.

Here are some exercises for those of you who speak too softly to help increase and control your volume. Practice them until you find it easy to do this.

EXERCISES FOR CONTROLLING LOUDNESS[15]

1. Initiate an "ah" sound in a tone which is barely audible, gradually increasing the loudness of the "ah" until it is louder than your usual conversational voice. Then reduce the loudness until the tone is again barely audible. Do not change the pitch or force the length of exhalation beyond a point of comfort.

2. Count from one to five increasing the loudness on each number. Begin with a barely audible "one" and end with a "five" which can easily be heard across a forty-foot room.

3. Count to seven, increasing the loudness up to four and then decreasing the loudness from five through seven. Maintain the same pitch level throughout the count.

4. Say each of the following phrases or sentence three times, increasing loudness from a normal conversational level to one which can easily be heard across a forty-foot room.

a. I'll go
b. Come back!
c. Please!
d. No!
e. I won't!
f. Enough!
g. Who's there?

5. Read each of the following sentences, first in an ordinary conversational tone and then as if you were trying to address a person in the tenth row of a crowded room.

a. I'll go in a few minutes.

b. The time is now.

c. I'll say this for the last time.

d. Listen if you wish to understand.

e. Are you John Jones?

These exercises should be helpful in overcoming the fear response with speaking loud enough to make yourself heard. Practice these exercises several times until you feel that you are speaking in a reasonably loud manner.

Social Skill #16: Speech Fluency. Like loudness of speech, the fluency with which you talk can make quite a difference with regard to either appearing confident and at ease, or sounding tense or shy. Speech fluency refers to the ability to speak easily and expressively, with a minimum of awkward pauses, and other fillers that tend to suggest social discomfort. How fluent is *your* speech? Ask yourself:

Is my speech pleasant to hear?

Do I effectively communicate my intent in both content and feeling?

Does my speech reflect me as I am?

How would I respond to someone whose speech was like mine?

Do I frequently pause or stumble in the middle of saying something?

Do I repeat myself often?

How often do I use expletives, like "umm," "uhh" and "Ahh"?

How can I improve the sound of my speech?

Fluent speech doesn't come naturally to many of us; it's something we have to work at, concentrating on the image we're projecting with the way we talk. Your answers to the above questions will tell you what you need to achieve this. The use of a tape recorder is also helpful—you can hear your progress—as you work to make your speaking more fluent and smooth.

Like the sound of our voice—its volume and the fluency of our speech—the way we *look,* move and carry ourselves, reflects our social attitude, communicating to others feelings ranging from insecurity, meekness, timidity, guilt and anxiety to pride, integrity, confidence and self-assurance. The last four skill areas we'll discuss have to do with this, the "body language" aspect of social interaction, with an emphasis on how social anxiety is communicated through our *non*-spoken behavior.

Social Skill #17: Eye Contact. One of the most obvious signs of social anxiety is a lack of *eye-contact* when talking or listening to someone else. If we're uneasy or self-conscious, it's hard to look someone in the eye while talking or listening to them. Instead, we tend to look away, toward the ceiling, floor, walls, our lap—anywhere except in that perilous straight line leading to the other person's eyes. After doing this for some time, we get used to looking away in social contact, and it becomes an anxious habit that's difficult to break.

How's *your* eye-contact? Do you maintain eye-contact during exchanges, or find yourself intensely studying the small clouds in your finger nails, the intricate face on your watch, the texture of the wall, the wine-stains on your lapel?

If you *do* tend to have poor eye-contact, work toward trying to improve it. As with the other skills, start with small steps, short periods of eye-contact, gradually lengthening them to the point where you no longer try to avoid it.

When you work on this skill, however, be careful not to *overdo* it, staring holes through the other person's retinas. Having someone maintain *100 percent* eye-contact makes many people nervous, and may turn them off. Eye-contact about *50 percent* of the time is probably what you want to shoot for here.

Social Skill #18: Posture And Other Movements. As you can see with a quick look at those around you, *posture* can reveal a great deal about how we feel. We convey our attitudes by how we move and carry our bodies. A straight, flexible posture communicates confidence and pride, while stooped shoulders and a lowered head conveys just the opposite.

In the same way, we can show anxiety by the little, unconscious acts we do, things we're often not even aware of. Like steadily jiggling or tapping your foot, or bouncing a leg up and down, drumming the fingers, clasping the hands, crossing the arms, shifting your weight constantly from one leg to the other, and so on.

So be aware of your *own* body-behavior. If you find yourself constantly doing these kinds of things, concentrate on shortening the amount of time spent this way, or get rid of them altogether.

Social Skill #19: Distance From Others. Probably as a behavioral leftover from our more primitive days, the *distance* we stand or sit away from others can make a difference in how they interact with us. Each culture seems to have its own unspoken rules or guidelines for this, but you can easily watch the effect this has on others. Standing too close may make a person uncomfortable, and he or she might well back off a bit. Too far away, and they may come closer in, or get a message saying that you're timid and may fear social contact.

How do you know the right distance? By simply watching others. How close together do *they* stand? What do the various distances they keep with others show about their relationships?

You can learn a lot of interesting things about effective and not-so-effective social responses by watching others. And if you find it necessary, change your behavior accordingly.

Social Skill #20: Facial Expression. "Facial Talk," a term also originated by psychologist Andrew Salter,[16] refers to the expression of your emotions, thoughts, and feelings through the use of your face. Many of us, especially the socially anxious, tend to hide what we feel behind a "mask," an unchanging, seemingly cold, insensitive, blank face with nary a smile, grimace, or furrowed brow. A *silent* face.

Letting your face talk, along with your mouth, offers you wide flexibility in showing your emotions, your feelings, what you're thinking, and increases your range of communications. If you're happy, *smile*. Angry? Let your face show it.

You may have trouble with facial talk at first, particularly if you've kept your face silent until now. If you do, try starting out practicing *over*-expression— exaggerate your facial distortion. If you're mad, for example, growl, squint your eyes and furrow your brows. If you're happy, let your whole face light up like Caesar's Palace on a clear night. Surprised? Act like you've just sat on a tack. Do the same thing with all the other emotions you feel, too.

Later, once you've got the hang of it, start toning down your facial talk until it looks appropriate, relative to your social community. As you progress with this, you'll notice how much facial talk adds to communication, both in yourself and others.

YOUR FIGHT AGAINST FEAR

We've just covered 20 different behaviors that are involved in effective social exchanges. Skills that will, *if you learn and use them,* help immensely in overcoming social fear, feelings of social inadequacy or inferiority, shyness, timidity and self-consciousness.

Even though it's impossible for us to tell you exactly what *you* need to do to conquer *your* specific fears, we feel confident that if you learn and *apply* to techniques presented in Chapters Five through Eight, your fears will be lessened, maybe by a little, perhaps by a lot.

With regard to social fear, don't try to rush through these various skills. Polish each one as you move along, gradually, making sure you've mastered the simpler ones before going to the complex, concentrating on remaining *relaxed* and calm as you slowly begin to use these skills more and more in your everyday life. If you find this hard, discovering that you're still becoming overly anxious, refer back to the previous chapters to aid in developing better, stronger controls over your arousal. Remember, fears usually have several sources, so a *combination* of the techniques we've presented throughout the book will very likely be your best bet if you run into problems.

And *persevere*. Hang in, because fear isn't a pushover in any case. The longer it's been with you, the longer it'll take to overcome. In fact, for many folks, getting the edge on fear and keeping it down becomes a *life-long* project; a continual course of action against unnecessary anxiety, arousal and discomfort; an endless effort to prevent new fears from growing. To be successful at breaking the fear response, we have to change the way we act, what we think, what we feel, developing a new consciousness, behavioral repertoire, and life-style immune to the anxiety and fear that's becoming so rampant in our society. And this new stance, if we succeed in getting there, will pay off in less discomfort, a longer life, better health, concentration and productivity, and a more meaningful, rewarding social exchange.

CHAPTER **NINE**

PROBLEMS, SOLUTIONS, AND CONCLUSIONS

We've attempted to give you ideas and techniques, exercises and encouragement to help you develop *your own*, personalized program for cutting down the unrealistic fears you've had knocking on your door. We've tried to guide you through the various procedures, showing, when we could, ways of combining techniques to conquer particularly stubborn arousal, like coupling SD and the learning of new social skills to decrease anxiety felt in certain interpersonal situations.

But sometimes, even the best laid plans produce results that are somewhat less than what we desire, a bit under our expectations. And the set of techniques we've covered, although quite effective for a wide range of arousal problems, *isn't* an all-powerful cure-all. Like anything else, these procedures have their limits.

So let's take a look at some of the things that can go wrong—or potentially lend themselves to interfering with your progress—so that you might be able to sidestep the holes in your program before falling into them.

PERVASIVE FEAR

One major troublemaker that may crop up is having difficulty in achieving a state of complete muscle relaxation. If you don't learn and consistently practice these exercises (see Chapter Five), you won't have an effective antistress response to use in countering arousal when it starts to swell in your innards.

To assess your degree of relaxation, look at how you feel after finishing your exercises. Ask yourself these questions:

Do I feel a complete absence of muscle tension in all parts of my body?

Do my arms, legs, hands and feet feel warm and heavy?

Do I feel nice and warm and heavy all over, sometimes to the point that I nearly dose off?

Am I letting my thoughts, particularly those that bother me, drift from my mind, replacing them with peaceful, pleasant thoughts?

Do I give myself enough time to enjoy the deeply relaxed state for at least ten minutes?

Am I making use of imagery (see Chapter Six, Teachnique C) to further enhance my relaxation experience?

If you answered *no* to any of these questions, go back and practice the exercises and techniques involved, working them into your everyday routine, until you can answer *yes*. Poor relaxation will undermine most of the procedures we've talked about in the course of the book, and it's important to remember that.

Some types of foods can make you feel nervous and edgy if your diet is too heavily laden with them, making you feel tense in spite of your attempts at staying relaxed. Things like candy, sugar, and other food and drink high in carbohydrates. In the same way, including too little or too much of certain vitamins and minerals in your daily diet can contribute to an edgy feeling.

Caffeine and nicotine are two commonly consumed drugs that operate along the same vein, making you feel anxious when you overdo them. Cigarette smoking causes a relatively immediate (within *three seconds* from the first puff) change in your system, the nicotine in the smoke jacking up your heart rate and blood pressure. And this spells arousal. When combined with the caffeine in five or six cups of tea or coffee or several glasses of soda pop (also high in caffeine), this can make you buzz along like a bee in honey shop.

So if you have a hard time relaxing, and smoke, drink coffee or both, try cutting back a bit and see the difference it makes. It may be a big one.

Some prescription drugs, such as "appetite suppressants" or "diet pills," can act as stimulants, increasing internal arousal despite your efforts at relaxing. If you feel that medication you're taking may be having this side effect, talk to your physician about it. He or she may be able to give you another type of medication that does the same thing without making you tense.

Someone might not want to shed a difficulty if it gets them sympathy or allows them to escape responsibility. Fact is, one person's problem is another's "blessing," helping them avoid going to work, run from aversive scenes, or get pity and attention they don't normally have. So, some prefer, usually unconsciously, to stay uptight rather than rid themselves of their problem and the payola it provides. We call these problem-related rewards *secondary gain*.

Think of a person whose pervasive, ever-present anxiety keeps him or her from working, a situation that's not all that uncommon. In cases like this, we may well find instances of what's known to psychologists as "symptom substitution." Based on the medical view of behavior problems which sees them as "symptoms" of some deeply rooted, underlying "mental disease," this refers to situations where once a problem is dealt with and disappears, another crops up in its place, serving as a grim reminder that all is *still* not well. In other words, all you've done is get rid of the behavior (symptom) while failing to solve the hypothesized under-lying "conflict" (illness).

If there's secondary gain present, we may well find a return of the anxiety, or some other problem. But not for the reasons the medical-model leads us to think, but rather because by eliminating the difficulty, we've also stopped the flow of pay-off it produced. In these situations, it's a good idea to learn other, more adaptive and worthwhile behaviors that produce rewards to avoid the recurrence of a problem.

If *your* program isn't doing what is should, take a close look at your motives. Your prospect for change may not be all that good if motivation is low, secondary gains high, and the chance to cop-out from responsibilities is present.

SYSTEMATIC DESENSITIZATION

Problems in relaxation can really hinder your beating a phobic fear. But if you absolutely *can't* achieve deep relaxation, there are other options to use in SD. The use of *anger* instead of relaxation, for instance, or *sexual* arousal. Both are incompatible with a fear state, and will work to counter it.

The reason deep muscle relaxation is the most common method is probably because most folks learn it fast and can stay relaxed over the length of a session pretty easily. Maintaining anger for that long is a different story. But if, even after a lot of hard practice you aren't able to make it work for you, and you've eliminated the possibility that something else is responsible, like your diet, habits, drugs or a medical problem, try anger or sexual arousal instead of relaxation. Other than the state being used to counter the anxiety, the procedure is exactly the same.

We mentioned in chapter seven that good, vivid,

clean imagery is important for SD to be effective. That's because it's based on the premise that you'll react to the imagined scenes in pretty much the same way you'd react to the real ones. So not being able to imagine clearly can really throw a wrench into the works. But if you can't see well through the eyes of your imagination, (and some people can't) there're still two options left open for you to use.

The *in-vivo* ("live") SD technique uses real fear stimuli in gradual steps rather than imagined ones, so imagery is bypassed. Take a fear of dogs, for instance: The dog-phobic would relax as fully and deeply as possible, and then look at a dog from, say fifty feet away. This distance is slowly reduced, just like in a hierarchy, to forty-five feet, forty feet and so on, until the person can actually touch the animal without fear.

In-vivo SD, however, can be a trifle difficult, or expensive depending on what the particular fear is.

Another option to standard SD is to use video taped, filmed, or photographed scenes, rather than live ones. This technique, called *in-vitro* SD, allows a lot more flexibility in hierarchy development than in-vivo SD affords, and it still doesn't require imagery.

A third problem that can result in SD not working is progressing through the scenes *too quickly*, leaving a particular item for the next one before you can really confront it *without becoming aroused*.

The simple solution to this problem is just to *slow down*. Zipping through the scenes while they still cause you fear isn't going to get you anywhere. Let your body be your guide. If you start feeling anxious while imagining (or watching) a scene, stop and regain a totally relaxed state before starting up again.

Hierarchies can also be a source of trouble. Take a look at yours: Are there at least *ten* items? Are the items separated by *less than 10* suds, preferably 5 for the last few scenes? Are the scenes described vividly enough for you to quickly and clearly imagine them? Do the scenes realistically illustrate your particular phobia? If not, your hierarchy might be the culprit.

Go back and review the instructions for building hierarchies (Chapter Seven). Check yours to see if a slight revision might help.

The possibility of secondary gain casts a bigger shadow on phobias than it does on pervasive fear. Take the pilot who suddenly develops a fear of flying. Or the door-to-door salesman who comes down with an intense fear of strangers. Their phobic fear would obviously screw up their jobs, probably keeping them out of work altogether. Depending on the tensions on the job, this may be a "blessing," making it a hard nut to crack.

If your self-directed SD isn't working, ask yourself this: Do I have anything to gain by *keeping* my phobia? Anything to lose by overcoming it?

If so, this is something you'll have to deal with before any program for the phobic fear will work.

Finally, SD may not be effective because the fear *isn't phobic*. For SD to work, the fear has to be centered around a specific, relatively concrete, thing, event, or situation. If your fear is pervasive, vague, or general, SD won't get rid of it.

Take a look at your fear, and make sure that it's actually phobic. You might want to review Chapter One to help you decide. Check to make sure your hierarchy items accurately cover what causes your fear response. If you have doubts, review the section on pervasive and social fears to determine whether these techniques might be more appropriate to your particular arousal difficulty.

SOCIAL ANXIETY

The thing that probably undermines more social anxiety programs than any other factor is not practicing new skills, and not using them in day-to-day life. Sure, it's not too difficult to learn how to start conversations the real challenge is *doing* it.

Reading about a new skill doesn't do you a bit of good unless you *learn* it, *rehearse* it and *try it out*, using it over and over until it becomes part of your spontaneous behavior. The kind of response that you make without thinking about it, one that doen't make you nervous, self-conscious, or flustered. This is the only way to overcome social anxiety. *Not* trying new responses out is just another form of avoidance, an escape that'll work to keep you firmly entrenched in the rut of fear, widening the social gap between you and others and increasing feelings of loneliness, despair and incompetence.

If you get a little anxious about trying something new (and who doesn't?), sit back and relax. If you're still unable to do it, write out an SD hierarchy that covers the situation—making small talk with others, starting a conversation, or whatever. Then, once you're able to *imagine* doing it without becoming anxious, go ahead and try it out.

As with pervasive fear and phobic anxiety, the ability to achieve good, solid relaxation is important in conquering social fear. But since we've already discussed this issue, we needn't belabor the point here.

If, after repeatedly rehearsing your skills, you continue to stay tense and apprehensive, there's probably an element of pervasive anxiety to your fears. Look back over Chapters Five and Six for ways to reduce this.

If you can't get relaxed, talk to your physician about it. It may be due to some of the health and/or diet factors we mentioned earlier.

OTHER PEOPLE'S REACTIONS TO THE NEW YOU

You know those little plastic puzzles with flat, sliding numbered squares all out of order? You have to push those little squares around until you have all the numbers in the right sequence. It looks easy until you pick it up and see that when you move one square, if affects all the other squares, making them hard to move where you want them.

It's the same with people. When we change, it can affect all those around us. And depending on how we've changed, they may have to adjust to new ways of responding to us. Like when we learn new social behaviors.

Let's take David Smith, our socially anxious friend from the first chapter. Before overcoming his social fears, David was very quiet, shy, timid, always going out of his way to do everything anyone asked, even when he didn't want to, never standing up for his rights as a human being. But as he began to learn new, more effective ways or relating to others and started shedding those fears, he noticed a change in his roommate. Let's look in on a conversation, and you'll

David walked home feeling tired. It had been a busy day and he was glad it was finally over.

Walking through the apartment door, he saw that the living room, as usualy, was in shambles. His roommate, Rick, had obviously had friends over—there were beer cans strewn about, bags of chips spilled, ashtrays overflowing with butts.

Just then, Rick came out of his bedroom, heading toward the door.

"Hey, David, how's it going? Listen, could you clean up a bit? I've got a date tonight and the place is a little trashed out. Be back later. . ."

"Hold it, Rick," David said. Rick stopped in mid-step, turning to look at David, a quizzical expression on his face. "I didn't mess up this place, you did. I'm not going to clean it up by myself. If you're in a hurry, maybe I'll help you, but I'm not going to clean it up by myself."

Rick just stood with his mouth open. David had never said "no" to a request before; he cleaned up the house nearly everyday by himself. What the hell was going

on, anyway?

David smiled inwardly at Rick's confusion, feeling a returning sense of pride in himself. It was kind of a new feeling, but one somehow strangely familiar, like when he caught that big fish up north, and his father had been so proud of him he didn't stop talking about it for a week.

When someone is faced with a change like David's, they may try to handle it with aggression, attempting to intimidate the formerly passive person back into his or her old role. Here's Rick's response:

"Look, damn it, clean up the house! You live in it, too, and mess it up as much as I do. You're nothing but a lazy slob, anyway. If you don't clean up this joint, I'll just have to find another roommate who's neater!"

Some folks, feeling the old fears starting to well up again, give in at this point, avoiding the confrontation, sliding back to their earlier modes of handling situations—compliance and passivity. But a better way to handle it is to stand your ground, face up to your apprehensions and stick with your answer. In David's case:

"Well, Rick, I'm sorry you feel that way, but it doesn't change the way I feel. I'm tired of doing all the work around here by myself. You messed up the living room, you clean it up. I'm not going to do it."

Chances are, the person will eventually realize you have changed, and adjust, recognizing your right to express your feelings and to refuse an unreasonable request. The important point for staying in control of your fears is remembering to stand your ground, while at the same time not letting the other person provoke you into being aggressive, too, if you can.

Further, some folks who can't handle the new you may try to coax you back to passivity through making you feel guilty about sticking up for youself. Example:

"Well, David, you know how much I like Cindy, and I just don't have time to straighten up and be there when

I told her I'd be. But I guess I'll have to be late. After all we've been through together, I'd hoped maybe you'd give me a hand. I guess you just don't like me. . . anymore. . ."

The use of guilt can be more powerful than a double-barrelled shotgun stuck in your back. People who use it effectively (and many do) will often succeed in making you feel like a worthless hound for not giving in, for not saying, "Okay, but *just this time!*" The problem is, it won't be just this time, but the next, and the next and the next after that. And once they've got you back in the old mold, its even harder to get out of it.

Even though it's difficult sometimes, the best strategy—in terms of staying on top of the situation—is to recognize their feelings, but once again stick to your guns. Consider David's response:

"You know, Rick, my not cleaning up the place doesn't mean I don't like you. I do, but I'm still not going to do it. If this really bothers you, let's talk about it. But I'm tired of doing all the work, and I'm not going to do it anymore."

The question comes up, won't this *change* some of my friendships? The answer is *yes*, most likely. If people have known you only as a passive, fearful person, they may well react to your new posture, looking for a way to handle it. But ask yourself: Is this friendship worth my remaining passive and afraid of speaking my mind? Should I just climb back under the old bridge of fear, not rock the boat, and hope I won't go under? A real friend *will* adjust to your new freedom, reacting positively to your growth, encouraging it.

Remember, along with you standing up for your rights as a person, you'll also be more fun to be around—more relaxed, clam, self-assured and friendly, showing *positive* emotions and feelings, being more *yourself* than ever before. And *this* is what people like, more than someone they can control, run over, or flatten like a toad on the highway, anytime they feel like it.

These are just some general suggestions—you'll have to guide yourself as to how far you want to go with a given person, when and when *not* to express what you're thinking and feeling, disagree with someone, make a request, and so on. For instance, it wouldn't be wise to go up to your supervisors and tell them that you feel they're incompetent clods, even if that what you feel. But *you* make the choice, *not fear*. Your actions are under *your* control instead of being whisked this way and that by the capricious whims of anxiety. And that's a distinction that'll make a big difference in how you feel about yourself.

PROFESSIONAL ASSISTANCE

While the strategies and techniques we've discussed in this book are effective in helping you deal with many fear problems, we'd like to stress again that they're not appropriate for everything, or for everybody.

There are many cases where a person's fear is too intense, long-standing, or complicated to be effectively handled by a self-applied program.

If your anxiety difficulties aren't helped by your application of the techniques you've learned, and still bother you quite a bit, your best course of action is to consult a psychologist, counselor, or your physician for further assistance.

Their expertise and advice will no doubt help you deal more effectively with your problems, guiding you through whatever techniques he or she decides are appropriate.

CONCLUSIONS: STAYING ON TOP OF FEAR

Many of the techniques we've shown you here aren't exactly new. Some, like SD, have been around quite a while, used with countless people, with an endless variety of fear. SD has also been the subject of a great deal of research over the years, and still claims effectiveness with phobic anxiety. Ellis' rational-emotive techniques (Chapter Six, technique B) are also firmly established ways of dealing with human problems. Many of the details and strategies we've included stem from our own clinical experience in helping folks handle anxiety problems, and represent some of the best, most effective ways we know of for overcoming unrealistic fears.

We've laid them out in step-by-step format, and lodged the ball firmly in your hands. It's up to you to run with it. As we've said again and again throughout the book, your success (or failure) depends on your motivation, commitment and perseverence in carrying out your program.

You've learned your fears, over a span of weeks, months, or years, and can *un*learn them if you have the interest, desire and will to act on what you've picked up in these chapters. It's up to you.

Once you feel yourself gaining on your fears, don't let up. Stay with it, keeping on the alert for new sources of fears infringing on your territory. The goal is to develop a new posture, a way of feeling, thinking and acting, that increases your *resistance* to irrational fear, that creates an environment in which the seeds of fear can't take root and grow.

What does this amount to? Several things.

First, good physical health and the ability to exert control over your inner arousal. You can keep your health up, of course, by sticking to a good, solid diet, one that's nutritious, containing the various vitamins and minerals your body needs, and by avoiding the abuse of things that can stimulate arousal, such as high-calorie food and drink, coffee and tea, cigarettes, alcohol, and so on. You don't necessarily have to give them up altogether, but try to watch your intake. It's best for you to control *them*, rather than the other way around. Your physician or dietician can help you put a diet like this together.

Besides what you feed your body, what you do with it is also important. Regular exercises can do wonders in helping us stay healthy—jogging, tennis, handball, swimming, dancing, racquetball, you name it. Any sustained activity that makes you exert yourself over a period of time will not only strengthen your body and increase your stamina, but also work to *relax* you.

Keeping up with the relaxation technique is very important in holding down your fort against attack by arousal. As you continue to do them, you'll find yourself able to relax very quickly, nearly any place you want to. We suggest you practice them daily, even after reducing your fears.

Second, a positive, rational, optimistic mode of thinking aids us in sorting out the various crazy, off-the-wall things that happen in our daily adventures. It's not hard for negative, depressing, anxiety-producing ways of thinking to slip, into our consciousness and expand to the point where we start to doubt ourselves, our competence, our ability to handle problems, once again clearing a path through which fear and self-doubt can walk, leaving us right back where we started.

When you begin to feel overly upset or anxious about something, take a look at what you're *thinking*. Is your concern or fear being fed by negative or irrational thoughts and beliefs? Being fostered and encouraged by unrealistic expectations or the way you're looking at the situation?

Of all the techniques we've talked about, keeping ahead of negative, irrational patterns of thinking is probably the hardest; and with some folks, it'll take more effort than with others. But it's well worth it. You may find that rational, positive thinking is the best way to put clarity and sense into rather muddy, nonsensical situations.

Third, it's important to be aware of what you do, how you act, particularly in a fearful or anxiety-producing situation. Are you running from it, or staying, fighting your anxiety with the weapons we've tried to give you? Unless you face your fears *head-on*, they'll get the best of you every time.

With social fears, keep practicing those skills you find the hardest, using them whenever you can in your interactions, *especially* if you start to feel tense. Launch an *active* attack on fear, rather than letting it roll over you. The more you stand up to fear by interacting, sticking up for yourself, expressing your feelings and emotions, the faster and more completely you'll break free of the inhibitions and discomfort it's caused you; and the better you'll be able to *stay* on top.

We're not promising you complete freedom, unconditional immunity from ever feeling the twinges of unrealistic fear again. That's probably impossible. But we are saying that by combining the various ways of *feeling, thinking* and *doing*, using what we've shown you, you'll have tools that'll make it easier to handle those you have and the ones that may crop up in the future.

In our experience with self-directed programs, we've found that people who help themselves get over a problem almost invariably receive an extra benefit when they're successful at it: A growing belief and confidence in themselves and in their new ability to deal with life's difficulties.

And isn't *that* what it's really all about?

APPENDIX 1

DARKNESS

1. You're at a friend's house, visiting in the late afternoon.
2. Before you know it, darkness has begun to fall. You decide to leave for home.
3. Walking down a well-lit street, you notice that darkness is approaching rather quickly. You realize that the sky will probably be completely dark before you arrive home.
4. As you continue, the streetlights become further apart. The night is approaching, and you find yourself walking into relatively large shadows between the lights.
5. As you arrive home, it's almost totally dark. You enter your living room in the dark and turn on the overhead light. You turn on the television.
6. You're in the living room watching television. The room is now lit only by a small lamp.
7. You're in the living room. The only light in the room is the glow from the television screen.
8. Going into the back of your garage to search for something you left there, you turn on the overhead light. As you search, the lightbulb burns out, plunging the garage into total darkness. After stumbling over several objects in the dark, you find your way out.
9. You're lying in bed, the room illuminated only by two candles.
10. You're lying in bed, the room totally dark.
11. You're walking down an unlit street on a dark, starless night with only a small flashlight illuminating your way.
12. Your flashlight breaks, leaving you in total darkness. You gradually make your way home through the dark.
13. While at a party, a lightning storm causes a power failure. All the lights in the house go off abruptly, leaving the party in total darkness. You wait patiently in the inky blackness for several moments until the lights come back on. You feel proud of yourself for remaining calm despite being in a totally dark room for several minutes.

EXAMS

1. You're relaxing at home, and you begin thinking about a series of exams you will be taking in four months.
2. The exams are now three months away.
3. It's now two months before the exams.
4. It's now one month before the exams. You've read the material to be covered by the tests, and are now beginning to study it more carefully.
5. The exams are now three weeks away.
6. The exams are two weeks away.
7. It's one week before the exams.
8. It's three days before the exams. You've studied the material closely, but continue to go over it to make sure you understand it all.
9. It's now the day before the exams. You're still going over your notes, and feel confident that you know the material.
10. It's now the morning of the exams.
11. It's one hour before the exams.
12. You're now entering the building where the exams are to be given. Even though you've studied the material carefully, you're beginning to feel slightly doubtful about knowing it well.
13. Ten minutes before the exams start, you're waiting outside the testing room. Another person waiting to take the test asks you to explain something that was covered in the study material. You find that you can only vaguely remember reading that material, and can't explain it to the person.
14. You enter the testing room and sit down to wait for the exam to be handed out.
15. The examiner comes in and starts passing out the exams. You receive yours, and begin to read over it.
16. As you begin answering the questions, you come to one you can't answer.
17. As you progress through the test, you find several other questions you have difficulty answering.
18. After completing the exam, you read your answers. You change some of them, and see several others you're not sure of.

19. You turn in your exam with the uneasy feeling of not knowing how you did on it. Nonetheless, you're glad it's over, and you feel proud of your self for having completed it without panicking.

OPEN SPACES

1. You're in your apartment, and you look out the window. The other apartments are very close, and you can see the walls of the neighboring building.
2. Watching the television, you see a brief scene of a broad expanse of desert, with a group of people riding horses across it.
3. You're in a large ballroom filled with people dancing.
4. Still in the ballroom, you notice that about half of the people have left. The room is beginning to appear larger.
5. Three-quarters of the people have left the ballroom, and it now looks much larger and open.
6. Everyone has left the ballroom, and you look across the broad, expansive room.
7. You visit some friends in Arizona, and they pick you up at the airport. Riding in the car, you find that you're approaching a ridge.
8. Getting to the top of the ridge, you find yourself exposed to a view of an open valley, stretching for miles and miles.
9. The driver pulls to the side of the road and stops the car.
10. You get out and admire the view of the large, open expanse stretching out endlessly before you.

RIDING ON A BUS

1. You're at home watching television, calm and relaxed.
2. While watching the television, you see a bus on the movie. You begin thinking about riding the bus to work rather than driving, and about how much money it would save.
3. The next morning, you walk to the bus stop. You arrive ten minutes early, and stand, waiting for the bus.
4. You're waiting at the bus stop, five minutes before the bus is due, and people begin to walk up to wait for its arrival.

5. You're waiting at the bus stop with several other people, one minute before the bus is due.
6. You see the bus come around the corner and slow to a hissing stop in front of you.
7. You watch as several people board the bus, laughing and talking.
8. You walk up to the bus doors and begin to board.
9. You board the bus, giving the driver your fare.
10. Seeing an empty seat, you walk toward it.
11. As you're walking toward your seat, the bus starts jerkily, causing you to stumble into your seat.
12. You hear the loud whine of the engine and smell the diesel exhaust as the bus picks up speed. Looking out the window, you notice that the traffic around the bus is getting heavier.
13. The bus driver suddenly slams on the brakes in heavy traffic to avoid hitting a car, causing you to jerk forward in your seat. A car behind the bus screeches to a stop to keep from hitting the bus. Many people are looking around nervously.
14. The bus lets you off at your stop. You get off, feeling good about having taken the bus to work without becoming fearful.

CROWDS

1. Sitting at home, you consider going on a shopping trip downtown.
2. You leave your house and walk to the bus stop. When you arrive, you see that there're five other people waiting for the bus.
3. As you're waiting, five more people come up and stand waiting.
4. You're now waiting at the bus stop along with fifteen other people.
5. As the bus arrives, the waiting people swarm toward the door. Finally getting into the bus, you see that there's standing room only. You stand along with several other people. The air inside the bus in warm and stuffy.

6. Getting off the bus, you walk into a department store. You see a table of clothes on sale that you want to look at. There's a crowd of ten people looking at the clothes. You move to the table, edging your way through the group, and begin looking at the clothes.

7. As you're looking, another ten people crowd to the table, swarming around you to get to the clothes. There is a fair amount of jostling and pushing among the twenty people as they reach over you and each other to look at the merchandise.

8. You're going to see a first-run movie that's very popular in town. After buying your ticket, you wait in the lobby for the previous showing to end. There are about thirty other people also waiting in the lobby.

9. As show time approaches, the lobby becomes more crowded. Ten minutes before show time, there are fifty people with you in the lobby.

10. Five minutes before the show starts, you're standing in the middle of a crowd of one hundred and fifty people, the lobby's capacity. Outside the lobby, a large line has formed to get in. There are people all around you, pressing closer and closer to the entrance of the theater.

11. They open the theater doors and the crowd pushes toward them. You're in the middle, trying to get in the entrance, being bumped and jostled by a crowd of about seventy people. You realize that if there were a fire, you'd probably never be able to get out of the building without being trampled.

12. Once inside, you find a seat. Looking around, you see that every seat is taken, and people are lining the aisles and back of the theater. There are about three hundred people in the room.

BEING ALONE

1. You're walking down a crowded street with several friends.

2. You're walking down a crowded street with several friends, and some of them leave, two of them staying with you.

3. You're walking down a crowded street with two friends, and one leaves.

4. You're walking down a crowded street with one of your friends, and the friend leaves. You're now alone.
5. You're walking down the street by yourself, and you notice that the crowd on the sidewalk is beginning to thin out.
6. Walking down the street alone, you see that there are only about ten other people in sight.
7. Walking down the street, you see that there are only five other people in sight.
8. Turning a corner, you find only two other people in sight, about a half a block in front of you.
9. Walking down the street you see only one other person, about a block and a half ahead of you.
10. Walking down the street, you notice that there's nobody else in sight, and realize that you're completely alone.
11. You're sitting at home relaxing. Noticing how silent it is, you become aware of being completely alone.

CEMETERIES
1. You're watching a television show, relaxing at home.
2. A scene comes on, depicting a woman walking toward a cemetery.
3. She enters the cemetery, and walks among the graves, looking at the headstones. She stops at one, standing on the grave examining the stone closely.
4. You're walking down the street looking for a friend's house. You notice a large cemetery on the opposite side of the street. A hearse is pulling into the gates, followed by a black limosine and several other cars.
5. You see that your friend's house is also on the other side of the street, next to the cemetery. You cross the street and walk past the cemetery to the house.
6. Reaching the house, you find your friend sitting in the yard. You join her, and notice that the cemetery is in full view from where you're sitting. You can see the funeral procession that entered the cemetery earlier. A casket is being carried toward the open grave.
7. You receive a phone call informing you of the death of an elderly relative. The family requests that you be a pallbearer at the funeral.
8. It's the day of the funeral, and the procession is headed toward the cemetery. You're about one mile away from it.

9. The procession enters the cemetery. You look out the window of your car and see hundreds of gravestones. Reaching the gravesite, you and the other pallbearers carry the casket from the hearse to the open grave. You stand looking into the grave momentarily before setting the casket down on the holder.

11. Looking around, you see that you're in the middle of a sea of graves, new and old, a variety of different types of headstones.

12. As you start to leave the cemetery, your car gets a flat tire. It's late afternoon, and dusk is beginning to fall. You're still in the middle of the cemetery. You haven't got a spare tire, so you walk to the mausoleum to call a friend for a ride to a gas station.

13. Darkness is beginning to fall, and you go outside to wait.

14. It's amost totally dark. You look around you, seeing the outlines of the larger headstones eerily illuminated by the quickly dying light.

15. Your friend arrives, and you take your flat to a gas station. They fix the tire, and you take it back to the car. It's totally dark now, the only light being that of the moon. After replacing the tire, you take one last look at your relative's grave, now covered with fresh dirt and flowers. You suddenly realize that you're the only living person in the entire cemetery. It's totally silent, except for the faint rustling of the leaves and a few unusual sounds that you can't quite put your finger on.

STORMS

1. You're sitting outside on a pleasant, sunny day. Looking up, you see a hint of clouds on the horizon.

2. Later, you see a bank of fluffy, white clouds beginning to drift across the sun.

3. The clouds cover the sun, and are followed by a large bank of darker clouds. The wind is beginning to pick up a bit.

4. About three-quarters of the sky is now filled with dark storm clouds, and the wind is starting to blow harder. You decide to go inside.

5. Once inside, you see slight flashes of lightning in the far distance. You can just barely hear faint rumbles of thunder.

6. On the radio, you hear a severe thunderstorm warning. Looking outside, you notice that your car windows are open. You dart through the beginning rain to close them. As you get in the car it begins to rain harder. You notice that the sky is getting darker and darker, and the lightning is getting closer.

7. After closing the window, you run back toward the house. You see a succession of three bolts of sharp lightning, followed by loud blasts of thunder.

8. Once you're inside, it starts raining more heavily, and the wind picks up even more. The lightning is getting closer, and the thunder louder.

9. The wind is now gusting, blowing the rain against your windows. The sky is nearly black with storm clouds, and the lightning is striking about once a minute.

10. As you watch out the window, you see the rain coming down in sheets, being blown savagely against your windows with great force. The noise of the rain is quite loud. The wind is gusting at high speed, and the trees are being blown around wildly.

11. You see a bright flash of lightning light up your house, followed almost immediately by an ear-splitting roar of thunder. As you look outside, another flash of lightning strikes so close you can see where it hit. The sound of thunder is nearly deafening.

RIDING IN A CAR

1. You're sitting outside relaxing, enjoying a beautiful day.

2. You're sitting outside and a friend drives up his/her new car.

3. Your friend asks you to come over to look at the new car.

4. While looking at the car, you open the door to look at the interior.

5. While looking at the interior, you decide to try out the seat. You get in, leaving the door open, and stretch out in the comfortable, soft seat.

6. Your friend asks you if you'd like to go for a short ride in the new car.
7. You agree, and close the door, buckling the seat belt.
8. Your friend starts the engine, and lets it warm-up in the driveway.
9. Your friend slowly backs the car down the driveway and out into the street, which is free of traffic.
10. Your friend puts the car in drive and slowly begins to pull away.
11. You're traveling down the street at 30 miles per hour in very light traffic.
12. You're traveling down the street at 40 miles per hour, and the traffic is starting to get heavier.
13. Your friend pulls onto a larger street, increasing the speed to 50 miles per hour.
14. You're traveling down the road at 50 miles per hour, and the traffic is becoming quite heavy.
15. Your friend pulls onto a freeway, and increases the speed to 55 miles per hour.
16. You're traveling down the freeway at 55 miles per hour, and the traffic is very heavy. Another car passes you at high speed, blowing the horn loudly.
17. A car swerves in front of you, narrowly missing your friend's car, causing your friend to slam on the brakes abruptly.
18. Your friend exits from the freeway, but again has to slam on the brakes to avoid hitting a large dog that's running across the road. This puts the car into a brief skid, after which your friend gets the car back under control.

INJECTIONS
1. You're not feeling up to par, so you make an appointment with your physician for the afternoon.
2. After examining you, the doctor tells you that you'll have to have a small injection of antibiotic.
3. A nurse enters, and asks you to roll up your sleeve.
4. You watch the nurse as he prepares the injection. After selecting a small hypodermic syringe, he plunges the long, thin needle into the top of a small bottle. Slowly, he fills the syringe by drawing the solution through the needle.

5. After clearing the needle by squirting a bit of the fluid out of the tip, he wets a ball of sterile cotton with alcohol.

6. Standing next to you holding your upper arm, he scrubs a small area with the cotton. You feel the coolness of the alcohol against your skin, and smell the vapors as it evaporates.

7. The nurse deftly inserts the needle into the muscle of your upper arm, injecting the antibiotic. You can feel a burning sensation deep in your muscle that seems to spread all the way down your arm to your hand. The nurse removes the needle, and you notice a small drop of blood forming at the site of the injection. He then places a band-aid over the puncture.

8. During a routine physical you are required to give a blood sample, drawn by needle from the large vein that runs down the inner side of your arm. A nurse prepares the area by scrubbing it with alcohol.

9. She then encircles your upper arm with a short length of rubber tubing. As she tightens it, you see the veins in your arm begin to swell.

10. She picks up a large hypodermic syringe and starts to move it toward a bulging vein. You watch and the thick, sharp needle inches forward and begins pressing against your skin.

11. You feel a pricking sensation as the needle enters your arm. But it misses the vein. The nurse withdraws it, and thrusts it in a second time. This time the pinching feeling is sharper as you see the sharp tip of the needle pierce your vein.

12. Loosening the tubing around your arm, the nurse begins drawing a sample of blood from the vein. You watch as the thick, dark fluid slowly fills the syringe. All the while you feel a burning, pricking sensation from the needle sticking in your arm.

13. The syringe is now filled with blood. The nurse smoothly withdraws the needle from your vein, and you see a drop of blood forming at the puncture. She places a piece of cotton over the wound, and tells you to hold it there while bending your arm at the elbow.

14. The nurse removes the blood-spotted piece of cotton, and replaces it with a small band-aid. She holds the filled syringe before you for a moment while making a note in your chart, and then leaves the room.

GOING TO THE DOCTOR'S OFFICE

1. You're sitting at home, one day before an appointment with your doctor.
2. You're in the car, driving to your doctor's office.
3. You've parked the car, and are walking through the door into the waiting room. You check in with the nurse, and he/she tells you to have a seat.
4. Sitting down, you pick up a magazine and start thumbing through it. You see that it's a nursing magazine that has several advertisements for medical equipment. As you look through it, you can faintly smell the odor of antiseptic in the air.
5. The nurse calls you in. Leading you to a small examining room, he/she tells you that the doctor will be with you in just a few minutes.
6. You sit in the small room, looking at the large examining table that takes up most of its space. You begin noticing several charts on the walls depicting a variety of disease symptoms. The smell of antiseptic permeates the room.
7. The doctor comes in, says "hello," and asks how you've been feeling.
8. The doctor asks you to remove your shirt (blouse), and places a stethoscope on your chest. You feel the cold metal against your skin.
9. The doctor moves the stethoscope to your back, asking you to breathe deeply and slowly. As you breathe, the doctor murmurs, "Hmmmmmm. . . " and asks if you've ever had trouble breathing.
10. The doctor then asks you to open your mouth, and places a tongue depressor on your tongue, asking you to say "Ahh. . ." You feel an urge to gag, as your tongue is held down. The doctor shines a light in your mouth, examining your throat for what seems like a long time.
11. The doctor now shines the light in your ears, saying "Hmmmmmm. . . ."

12. The doctor then looks at your chart, and begins making notes. You look around the room seeing a large array of medical apparatus, including thermometers, blood-pressure cuffs and hypodermic syringes of various shapes and sizes.

13. The doctor writes out a prescription for some medicine, and tells you to make an appointment for next week.

14. The nurse hands you the bill and you leave.

RIDING IN A TRAIN

1. You're sitting at home relaxing, reading a book.

2. While sitting at home, you begin thinking about visiting some relatives across the state. You decide to take the trip by train.

3. You arrive at the train depot with your luggage, and sit to watch some trains come in.

4. You buy a round-trip ticket, and check your baggage. You sit down and wait for your train.

5. The announcement is made that your train is now ready for boarding. You approach the train.

6. You enter the train, giving your ticket to the conductor.

7. Looking down the coach car, you see it is quite crowded. You find your seat and sit down. Departure is scheduled for 10 minutes.

8. You're sitting in your seat five minutes before departure.

9. You're sitting in your seat one minute before departure.

10. You feel the train start with a jerk that pushes you back into your seat.

11. You look out the window as the train begins to gain speed. You can feel the wheels rumbling beneath you as the train starts going faster and faster.

12. As the train reaches cruising speed, you sit back to read a newspaper. On the front page you see a story about a train wreck in which several people were killed.

13. You read the article and relax in your seat, watching the scenery through the windows as your train rolls toward its destination.

BEING WATCHED

1. Walking outside of your house and saying hello to your neighbors.
2. Walking down the street and exchanging greetings with the postman.
3. As you walk by a large crowd of people waiting for a bus, you trip and they stare at you.
4. As you walk into a crowded supermarket, you notice that the people waiting to be checked out are staring at you.
5. In the supermarket as you are trying to pull out a grocery cart that is stuck, everyone is watching you.
6. Dropping a large jar of pickles, everybody in the store stares at you.
7. Walking into a large crowded department store, you drop your coat and all of the other people in the store stare at you.
8. When you are checking out in a crowded line, the clerk overcharges you. You bring this to her attention as the crowded line watches.
9. You are at work, and several fellow workers are standing behind you and watching you work.
10. Your supervisor joins the gathering of fellow workers, and they are all watching you work.
11. Making a mistake at work with your supervisor bringing it to your attention. There is a crowd of fellow employees looking on, and they are laughing.

ELEVATORS

1. Walking toward a tall building you comtemplate using an elevator.
2. Entering tall building you look at elevator as you decide to use it.
3. Walking toward elevator 20 feet away.
4. Walking toward elevator 10 feet away.
5. Walking up to elevator and standing next to closed door of shaft.
6. Pushing elevator button for elevator to come from another floor.
7. Hearing whosh of elevator as it decends to your floor.

8. Elevator now at your floor and door getting ready to open.
9. Door of elevator opens and you look inside of elevator.
10. You walk into elevator.
11. Standing inside elevator you push button for next floor above.
12. Door closes and elevator ascends to next floor.
13. Door of elevator opens and you get off feeling good with self.
14. You move over to next shaft and, after awaiting an elevator, you enter.
15. Door closes and push button for the 16th floor which is fifteen floors above you.
16. Alone in elevator as it ascends fifteen floors.
17. Elevator reaches the sixteenth floor and you walk out feeling very pleased with yourself for having used the elevator.

FLYING

1. Reading an ad in newspaper about reduced air rates to a Pacific island resort.
2. Thinking about flying to above island—three weeks from flight time.
3. Deciding to purchase airplane tickets for vacation. Two weeks from flight time.
4. Going to travel office and paying for and picking up tickets - two weeks from flight time.
5. At home thinking about flight to resort island - one week away.
6. At home thinking about upcoming flight and vacation—five days away.
7. At home thinking about upcoming flight and vacation—four days away.
8. At home thinking about upcoming vacation—three days away.
9. It is now two days before flight time—at home thinking about vacation.
10. Day before vacation flight.
11. Day of flight—leaving home and driving toward airport.

12. Parking car in terminal lot and watching airplanes.
13. Walking toward terminal.
14. Walking into terminal and heading toward ticket counter.
15. Walking up to ticket counter and checking in with agent.
16. Walking to the gate the flight's departing from, and passing through the security check.
17. Waiting to board plane—looking at it through window.
18. Getting ready to board plane—walking down ramp to enter plane.
19. Actually walking into plane.
20. Being seated in seat next to aisle.
21. Strapping self down and hearing pilot talk about upcoming flight.
22. Feeling engine vibration and hearing engine noise.
23. Plane is taxiing toward takeoff point.
24. Engines race as plane prepares to take off.
25. Plane races down runway and nose begins to lift off.
26. Plane is airborne and climbing.
27. Plane is cruising at flight altitude—you can hear engine noise and feel slight vibrations.
28. You unsnap seat belt, lean back and relax—stretch your legs and relax completely—pleased with yourself.
29. Approaching destination, you fasten seatbelt, plane begins descent pattern.
30. Plane prepares to land.
31. Plane actually lands—you feel bump and engines race backwards to brake plane.
32. Walking off plane you feel very pleased with self for having flown.

MAKING A PUBLIC SPEECH

1. Receiving invitation to express your views publicly concerning a new park for your community.
2. Deciding to accept invitation.
3. One week before time you are to express your view.
4. Five days before speech—you make a short five-minute speech covering what you want to say and practice it, remaining relaxed while imagining you are standing before group.

5. Four days before speech time and you are continuing to practice speech before imagined group.
6. Three days before speech time and you continue to practice speech.
7. Two days before speech time as you continue practicing speech.
8. Day of speech and you have practiced your speech at least ten times.
9. Five hours before speech time.
10. One hour before speech time—you prepare to arrive at meeting hall where discussions are to be held.
11. Driving toward meeting hall.
12. Pulling up and parking in lot beside meeting hall.
13. Walking toward meeting hall.
14. Entering meeting hall and seeing all the people gathered there.
15. Listening to others make their brief speeches.
16. Five minutes before time for your speech.
17. Being called upon to give your speech.
18. Standing up from your seat in the meeting hall and getting ready to give speech.
19. Starting off by saying "Mr. Chairman, thank you for this opportunity to express my views. My name is _____ and I'd like to say. . ." Give speech.
20. As you are giving your speech you are experiencing a good feeling of confidence. You glance around the room and feel renewed confidence as you continue your speech.
21. Speech is over and you sit down feeling very pleased with yourself.

APPLYING FOR A JOB

1. Reading newspaper classified you see ad for a job you would like.
2. You call up number listed and are informed you will have to be interviewed the next afternoon at 4:00 PM You agree.
3. You hang up phone and think about pending job interview for next afternoon.

4. It is next morning—the day of the job application—and you think of the pending interview at 4:00 PM.
5. 11:00 AM and you think about pending interview.
6. 1:00 PM and you think of pending interview.
7. 2:00 PM and you think of pending interview.
8. 3:00 PM and you think of pending interview at 4:00 PM
9. Leaving your home and driving toward site of interview.
10. 3:45 PM — parking car in front of office building where interview is to be held.
11. 3:50 PM — walking into building.
12. Walking to suite where interview is to be held.
13. 3:55 PM — walking up to receptionist and identifying yourself and mentioning that you have a 4:00 PM appointment.
14. 3:57 PM — seated in reception room waiting to be called for interview.
15. 4:00 PM — you are asked to go into next room.
16. Entering next room you see a man standing beside his desk.
17. This man identifies himself and you say "Hello, I'm _____
18. This man starts his interview and you respond in a confident, comfortable way.
19. Interview over — you leave feeling very pleased with yourself.

WALKING INTO A ROOM FULL OF PEOPLE
1. You have been invited to a small party of a friend's house and you are standing in your home reading invitation.
2. After deciding to go, you call up friend and state you will be attending.
3. Getting dressed to leave for party.
4. Driving your car toward friend's house.
5. Turning onto street of friends house.
6. Driving down street and seeing friend's house with large number of cars in front.
7. Parking car and walking toward house.
8. Walking up to door and knocking.
9. Door opens and you see a room full of people.

10. Friend says he's glad you could come and opens door.
11. You walk into room full of people.
12. You are in middle of room full of people.
13. Standing in the middle of this room you feel relaxed and confident.
14. You turn to someone and introduce yourself saying "Hi, I'm _____
15. After making an introduction you then engage in small talk.
16. You spend the evening feeling pleased with yourself because you were able to approach others and make small talk.

FEAR OF LULL IN CONVERSATION
1. Walking down street alone.
2. Seeing group of people you casually know at a bus stop.
3. Walking up to group and exchanging greeting talk.
4. Making small talk for a short period of time.
5. You are standing in group when conversations begins to slow down.
6. People run out of things to talk about and remain silent.
7. You are in middle of group and no one has said anything for ten seconds.
8. You are in middle of group and no one has said anything for twenty seconds.
9. You are in middle of group and no one has said anything for thirty seconds.
10. You are in middle of group and no one has said anything for forty-five seconds.
11. You are in middle of group and no one has said anything for two minutes.
12. You are in middle of group feeling relaxed and at ease after ten minutes of silence.
13. Bus comes and you board bus feeling pleased with yourself for being able to tolerate silence.

FEAR OF CROSSING BRIDGES
1. Standing outside of home thinking about visiting a friend on the other side of a bridge.
2. Friend drives up and the two of you go for a ride to visit above friend.

3. Riding in car thinking about crossing bridge.
4. Your friend starts to take the two of you for a ride to the other side of the bridge to visit with friend.
5. Heading toward bridge ten blocks away.
6. Riding toward bridge eight blocks away.
7. Riding toward bridge six blocks away.
8. Riding toward bridge four blocks away.
9. Riding toward bridge two blocks away.
10. One block away from bridge — you can now see it.
11. Stop at red light looking at bridge one-half block away.
12. Driving up to enter ramp of bridge.
13. Leaving entrance ramp and actually starting to cross bridge.
14. One third of way across bridge.
15. One half way across bridge
16. Two thirds of way across bridge.
17. Other side of bridge with good feeling of satisfaction at having crossed it.

FEAR OF CROSSING STREETS

1. You are in your apartment thinking about going outside to street.
2. Getting ready to go outside.
3. Leaving apartment and walking down hallway.
4. Riding down elevator to lobby.
5. Door of elevator opens at first floor.
6. Walking into lobby.
7. Looking at door leading to street outside.
8. Walking toward street door.
9. Walking through street door.
10. Walking onto sidewalk in front of apartment building.
11. Looking down street to corner of block away.
12. Walking toward corner one block away.
13. Walking toward corner two-thirds of a block away.
14. Walking toward corner one-third of a block away.
15. Walking toward corner thirty feet away.
16. Walking toward corner ten feet away.
17. Standing at corner.
18. Standing at corner looking both ways and seeing no traffic.
19. Getting ready to cross street.

20. Walking across street.
21. Other side of street, feeling good — pleased with self at having crossed.

FEAR OF RIDING IN CROWDED SUBWAY

1. In the security and comfort of your home thinking about riding the subway.
2. Getting ready to leave home and go ride subway.
3. Leaving home and walking toward subway entrance.
4. Four blocks away from subway.
5. Three blocks away from subway.
6. One block away from subway seeing large number of people at entrance.
7. Walking up to crowded entrance.
8. Mingling with crowd at entrance to subway.
9. Walking in crowd toward subway.
10. Purchasing ticket at window.
11. Standing on the crowded subway platform.
12. Hearing subway train approaching.
13. Train stopping and people converging at entrance to train.
14. Joining crowd at entrance to subway train.
15. Doors of train opening and people beginning to enter.
16. You are entering subway train with many other people.
17. You are standing inside subway train and it is crowded.
18. Inside subway car standing up among people being jostled back and forth as train moves to next station.
19. Standing up in crowded car looking around and feeling relaxed.

STRANGERS

1. You're walking down a street with a friend on a bright sunny day.
2. You're walking with a friend, when a person you don't know stops you and asks for directions.
3. You're shopping at a mall and a stranger asks you for a donation to the religious group he is representing.
4. You go to visit a friend and find her there with three people you don't know. You sit down and are introduced to them.

5. You're riding in a bus and the person sitting next to you, a stranger, starts to strike up a conversation.
6. You're at a large party with two friends. Five strangers join you group. Your friends introduce you to them.
7. As you talk to these five people, you notice your friends have walked away, leaving you alone with them.
8. You're invited to a party by a friend. On arriving, you notice that you really don't know anyone there besides your friend. There are about twenty people at the party.
9. Your friend takes you around and introduces you to each of the strangers, and then leaves you alone with them.
10. Several of the strangers form a circle around you, and start asking you to tell them about yourself.
11. While at the party, you walk into a room filled with people. You look around and see that there's nobody there you know.
12. You walk into a bar with about 40 other people in it. Sitting down, you look around you and see that you don't know anyone in the place.

HARMLESS INSECTS*

1. You're sitting in a chair reading a book.
2. You're sitting in a chair, and you notice a small spider crawling down the wall about six feet away.
3. The spider crawls out onto the floor and begins moving toward you, about four feet away.
4. The spider continues toward you, and is now two feet away from your chair. You notice that it's larger than you thought.
5. The spider crawls up onto the chair, and is now about one foot from your arm.
6. It continues toward you arm, and is now only inches away. You can see its many legs moving in unison as it approaches you.
7. The spider moves onto your arm and stops momentarily. You regard it for a minute, and then flick it off your arm to the floor.
8. While walking through your garage, you run into a spider's web. As you brush it off, you notice a moderately-sized spider has remained on your arm. You feel it crawl quickly over your skin.

9. You're at a friend's place, and you feel something on your face. You brush your hand at it, and see that it's a relatively large spider. It falls from your face onto your leg.

10. While laying in bed you feel something crawling on you. Pulling the sheet down, you see it's a large spider. You brush the insect to the floor and return to sleep.

11. At a picnic, you're strolling through a wooded area. You walk into a large web, and several spiders fall on you—in your hair, on your face, and all over your bare arms. You calmly brush them off and return to the picnic.

*If your fear involves insects other than spiders, simply replace the spiders in the above scenes with the type(s) of insect you fear.

SWIMMING (OR WATER)

1. You're lying on a lounge at the side of a pool, relaxing in the sun.

2. You're sitting on the side of the pool, your feet dangling in the water, cool and refreshing.

3. You walk along the deck to the shallow end of the pool, and slowly walk down the steps into the water. The pool is three feet deep at this point, and the water feels cool and enjoyable.

4. You walk further out into the pool to where the water is four feet deep. You submerge yourself up to your neck, feeling the water surrounding you.

5. Standing in the five-foot-deep section of the pool, you submerge yourself completely for a moment. As your head goes under the water, you notice the relaxing experience of silence beneath the surface.

6. You push off from the bottom and swim to the other side of the pool, gliding easily through the water. You're now in water that's six feet deep.

7. Now over your head in the pool, you tread water.

8. You jump off a low diving board into water twelve feet deep. Rising to the surface, you swim to the side of the pool and remain there, treading water.

9. You're out in a small boat on a lake with some friends. The water is twenty feet deep. You dive in off the boat. After swimming awhile, you climb back into the boat, feeling cool and refreshed.

10. You're out in the ocean in a small boat with some friends. It's not far offshore, but the water beneath is over fifty feet deep. You dive into the water and swim with your friends.
11. You're quite a ways out in the ocean in a moderately sized cruiser. The water below is over one hundred feet deep. You dive in off the bow for a refreshing dip.

HARMLESS SNAKES

1. You're watching a movie on television. There's a scene showing a child playing on the lawn.
2. The scene shows the child watching a small snake crawling through the grass.
3. The child picks up the snake, and begins playing with it. She laughs as she plays.
4. While working in your garden with a friend, you see a small garter snake moving slowly, about six feet away.
5. The snake is moving closer, and is now about three feet away.
6. Your friend sees the snake and walks over to it, picking it up.
7. Holding it gently, stroking its head she approaches you, saying, "Look at this snake . . . isn't it pretty?" She's now about one foot from you, and you can see the snake's tongue flicking in and out of its mouth.
8. Your friend holds the snake out to you, and you reach over and stroke its head, feeling its dry, smooth, scaly hide.
9. Your friend hands the snake to you, and you hold it. It looks up at you, flicking its tongue as you stroke its head.
10. At a zoo, you watch a man handling a three-foot milk snake. Its rather large body is curled around his arm. He's standing about four feet from you, behind a chainlink fence.
11. The man pets the snake's large, scaly head, and you can see the snake's tongue flicking in and out. He's now about two feet from the fence.

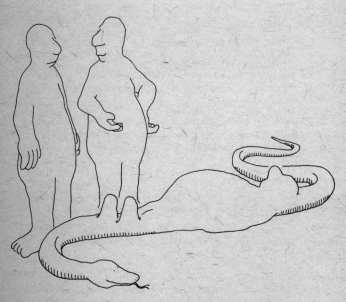

At least he proved he's no longer afraid of snakes!

12. He asks you if you'd like to touch the snake. You reach over the fence and stroke the snake's head, feeling its cool, smooth skin. It opens its mouth wide, and you see how large its jaws are, but notice it hasn't got fangs. Its tongue continues to flick in and out.
13. He hands you the snake, and you hold it, stroking it as it curls around your arm.
14. While working in the yard, you see a rather large garter snake. You walk up to it, picking it up. You watch it flicking its tongue as you gently stroke its head.

APPENDIX 2

SYSTEMATIC DESENSITIZATION CHECKLIST[17]

Name _____ Date _____

Specific Fear Response _____

Tasks	Date
1. Achieved skill in deep muscle relaxation	_____
2. Developed systematic desensitization hierarchy	_____
3. Checked hierarchy and made suggested or needed changes	_____
4. Developed ability to visualize scenes	_____

5. Record of systematic desensitization. Directions: Write the date and number of the session in the far left column, the number of the scene being visualized in the second column, and the number of times the scene was visualized in the third column. Record one scene per line. Indicate the level of discomfort produced during each visualization of any specific scene by writing in a number from 0 to 100 in the column on the far right. Zero means no discomfort, 100 means the highest degree of discomfort. Note: Each scene should be imagined enough times so that on its last visualization it produces *no* feeling of discomfort, or one no greater than *five* suds.

Date and Session Number	Scene Number	Number of Visualizations	Discomfort Level During Each Visualization (0 to 100 suds).

NOTES AND REFERENCES

1. The two examples of phobic fear are reprinted by permission from *Self-Directed Systematic Desensitization: A Guide for the Student, Client, and Therapist*, by W.W. Wenrich, H.H. Dawley, and Dale A. General. Copyright © 1976 by Behaviordelia, Inc. Kalamazoo.

2. Russek, H.L. and Zohman, B.L. (1958) Relative Significance of Heredity, Diet and Occupational Stress in Coronary Heart Disease in Young Adults, *American Journal of Medical Science, 235, 266-275.*

3. Sulzberger, M.B. and Witten, V.H. (1959) The Management of Acne Today, *Medical Clinics of North America*, 43, 887-902.

4. Blackwell, B. (1973) Psychotropic Drugs in Use Today; the Role of Diazepan in Medical Practice, *Journal of the American Medical Association,* 225: 1637-1641.

5. This section is taken from *Self-Directed Systematic Desensitization: A Guide for the Student, Client, and Therapist,* By W.W. Wenrich, H.H. Dawley, and Dale A. General. Copyright © 1976 by Behavirodelia Inc., Kalamazoo. Reprinted by permission.

6. Ibid

7. Young, M. (1979) unpublished Doctoral Dissertation University of Southern Mississippi.

8. Ibid

9. Ellis, A *Reason and Emotion in Psychotherapy.* New York: Lyle Stewart. Copyright © 1962 by Lyle Stewart. Reprinted by permission.

10. The remainder of this chapter is based on material taken from *Self-Directed Systematic Desensitization: A Guide for the Student, Client, and Therapist,* by W.W. Wenrich, H.H. Dawley, and Dale A. General. Copyright © 1976 by Behavirodelia, Inc. Kalamazoo. Reprinted by permission.

11. Wolpe, J. *Psychotherapy by Reciprocal Inhibition.* Stanford: Stanford University Press, 1958.

12. Rathus, S.A. (1973) A 30-item Schedule for Assessing Assertive Behavior, *Behavior Therapy,* 4, 398-406. Copyright © 1973 by Academic Press, Inc. Reprinted by permission.

13. The remainder of the chapter is paraphrased from material contained in *Achieving Assertive Behavior: A Guide to Assertive Training,* by H.H. Dawley and W.W. Wenrich. Copyright © 1976 by Wadsworth Publishing Company, Inc. Reprinted by permission.

14. Salter, A. *Conditioned Reflex Therapy.* New York: Farrar, Straus, 1949 Copyright © 1949, 1961 by Andrew Salter. The examples of "feeling talk" are reprinted by permission.

15. These exercises are taken from *The Improvement of Voice and Diction,* by J. Eisenson. Copyright © 1958 by Macmillan Publishing Co., Inc. Reprinted by permission.

16. Salter, A. *Conditioned Reflex Therapy.* New York: Farrar, Straus, 1949.

17. This checklist is taken from *Self-Directed Systematic Desensitization: A Guide for the Student, Client, and Therapist,* by W.W. Wenrich, H.H. Dawley, and Dale A. General. Copyright © 1976 by Behaviordelia, Inc. Reprinted by permission.